D1246245

Good Girlz With Hood Habits

By

Erica Dyer

ISBN 978-0-578-78005-4

Library of Congress Catalog Card Number 2020919752

Good Girlz With Hood Habits

Written by: Erica Dyer

Cover Design: GermanCreative

Website: www.ericareads.com

# Dedication

This book is dedicated to the men that taught me and the women that raised me.

William, Willie, Buddy, Morris, Purnell, and Mr. Dyer

Hazel, Joan, Arnetta, L'Tanya, Demetria, Faith, and Tara

This book is for y'all.

## Acknowledgments

To my Heavenly Father thank you for this gift and for the strength I needed to pursue this path.

To my family and friends thank you for the genuine support and love. To my co-workers that went from friends to family I thank you all for pushing me and believing in me more than I did myself.

Mr. Dyer, my heart outside my chest, I pray I've made you proud. No matter what, Mommie got you forever.

To my parents, I love y'all and am forever grateful.

Purnell, my brother, my oldest child. We have been rocking for 32 years. Even when you get on my last nerve, I still love you! Make this your last "vacation" screaming "free you" until it's "you free."

Tiff Piff, my sister, my ride or die, I love you! Thank you for being my ear, my shoulder, my eyes, and my diary.

My two Mira's, our sisterhood may not be perfect but you girls inspire me to go further and do better. My love for y'all runs deep. #ThemDyerKids

Willie Nelson my pop pop, you could have walked away years ago. I know it couldn't have been easy stepping in and stepping up but I thank God you did! I love and cherish you.

Last but not least I want to thank every bad relationship, friendship, and job that I ever had. It took me years to realize I had to let go of my hate towards y'all to receive my blessings.

This is just beginning.

**Something About Them "Green" Girls**

# Good Girlz With Hood Habits

Lalani Williams A.K.A Lay

I've always been a "good girl." I grew up trying to please everyone, from my parents to my brothers, to teachers; I never wanted to disappoint anyone. That's probably why I ended up in fucked up relationships and currently fighting Rico (Racketeer Influenced and Corrupt Organizations Act) charges. My story is the classic cliché of a good girl loving hood niggas.

My first real relationship was with my child's father. That nigga name should have been Ike Jr. because he whipped my ass every damn day for five years. I never got my brothers involved in my bull shit, and to this day, I regret that decision. Had I talked to anyone of them or told them the shit I was going through, maybe they could have helped me out. But no, I wanted to be so damn independent, now my dumb ass is someone's co-defendant and raising two children by myself. I guess I should start this from the beginning and show you how I went from a green goody two shoes to a scamming, drug smuggling, boss ass bitch.

# Good Girlz With Hood Habits

My name is Lalani Williams, I'm 24 years old, and I'm going to tell you how I went from a weak-minded little girl to a bossed-up bitch in a matter of almost three years. I have two children. My son is six, and my daughter is nine months old. They have two different fathers; both of them have nothing to do with my kids.

My son's father was my high school sweetheart turned nightmare. I met Si'on during my senior year in high school. I wasn't looking to be in a relationship. Hell, I was on my way to college with a full-ride scholarship. All I was trying to do was have a little fun before I left Baltimore. My homegirl invited me to a house party that this nigga Marty was having. He was a street nigga, a real money getting type boss nigga, but the only one out of his crew to graduate, so they went all out for him.

This nigga had strippers, hella food, an open bar, and the DJ was hitting. It was an all-white theme, so I rocked an all-white Adidas sweatsuit with a pair of white Balenciaga's. Yeah, I was getting money too. I worked part-time for an all you can eat restaurant near Eastpoint Mall, and I also bartended at my

# Good Girlz With Hood Habits

uncle's hole in the wall club some nights. At 16, I was seeing drug dealer money. My uncles made sure to look after me once my dad was killed three months after I was born. My dad was a kingpin on the eastside of Baltimore. He was gunned down in front of my grandmother's house by his side chick. Even after his death, my mother nor her kids wanted for anything. We weren't dripping in diamonds or anything like that, but we had all we needed and wanted. My dad's hustler spirit was embedded in me. I've been working since I was 14. I had $12k saved, and my bankroll was growing.

Getting back to the party. I was talking to this fine ass nigga named GM, but he was on some other shit; I guess he thought because he was flashing money all night, I would be down to fuck. Nigga, please! He ended up leaving not too long after I got there. That's when I met Si'. He was at the diner we went to after the party. He was with his two friends and was looking good. Si stepped to me, and the rest was history. I thought I had met my soulmate; it was like living on a cloud for the first three months that we were together. But as soon as I gave up the goods to his ass, he started beating my ass. At first, it was small little shit like pulling my hair if I got too smart, then he would pinch my legs, but after a while, he got downright dirty and started whipping my ass. Even while I was pregnant, he would smack me.

I never reached out and told anyone because I was so ashamed. He made me stop working at the club the second week we started messing with each other. He said I didn't need to be in the club late at night with a bunch of niggas staring me in my face. Now that I look back at it, he probably did that so my uncles wouldn't see the black eyes and busted lips.

I was supposed to go to the University of Maryland Eastern shore but stayed home and enrolled at Coppin State University to be with Si'on. That was the dumbest shit I ever did in life. I got pregnant three times by this nigga. The first two times, I miscarried due to getting my ass whipped. The last pregnancy, I was going to get rid of it, but Si' promised he would stop putting his hands on me. He did for the first six months, but that all ended the night of our baby shower. He got so drunk and started talking about I was cheating on him and that this wasn't his baby. I went to leave, and he fucked me up so bad that I went into labor early. My son was born at 32 weeks. Luckily, he was a healthy baby and only had to stay in the NICU for one month.

After that, I attempted to leave Si', but that was short-lived. No one knew the monster I was living with; I had nowhere to go with a newborn, or so I thought. Si' never knew about the money I had saved, nor did he know that once I turned 21, I would get access to my trust fund. I just had to make it to see 21 without this nigga killing me. I ended up dropping out of school in my second year and got a job as a Correctional Officer at one of the worst jails in the state of Maryland. I hated this fucking job with a passion. Too many niggas tried me. Every day it was some bull shit with administration, and I was sick and tired of it. I know my daddy was turning over in his grave at how his baby girl was living.

My family thought Si' was taking care of home, and I only worked because of boredom. Looking back, my family was pretty fucking stupid. Why the fuck would I work in a jail just to pass the time? Si' ass didn't work, and the little bit of money he did make selling weed went to his drinking and other bitches. I paid all the bills in the house, including the high ass rent in the damn apartment Si' just had to live in. Talking about, he couldn't have his seed living in the hood. We lived in Fells Point; our rent was $2,200 a month. My checks covered the rent, and my side hustle took care of the other bills. I started working back at my uncle's bar once my son turned two. Si' didn't know because I would lie and say I was working overtime at the jail. Long as money was coming in the house, he didn't give two flying fucks where I got it from.

"Bitch, you going make me kill your dumb ass."

"Si' I didn't do anything."

I'm not sure where that came from, I never talked to Si' like that, but I was getting sick of him treating me like a damn child or worse, a dog. We had just come from the mall, and some nigga tried to holla at me. But of course, bitch ass Si' didn't ask the nigga; he straight barked on me.

# Good Girlz With Hood Habits

"Oh, yeah Lay who the fuck you think you're talking to? You feeling yourself, aren't you?"

"No, Si', I'm sorry."

"Yeah, your ass is sorry, take your ass in the fucking room and don't bring your ass out."

"Si' your child's name is Harlem. I'm going to go wherever the fuck I want to go! I'm sick of this shit. You can't keep talking to me like that. I'm a grown-ass......"

Si' smacked me right in the face. I fell on the floor next to Harlem. However, the fact that his son was there watching him hit me didn't stop him from kicking me in my side, then dragging me by my hair to our room. I heard Harlem crying for Si' to stop hitting me, but of course, he didn't. Si' shut the door to our room and continued to hit me like his name was Mike Tyson. I begged him to stop, but he was determined to teach me a lesson. If the beating wasn't enough, this nigga had the nerve to rip my clothes off and fuck me. I continued to beg for him to stop, and he didn't.

"Bitch don't scream now; you wanted that nigga in the mall to fuck you, right? This what you wanted, take this dick and shut the fuck up."

"Si, please just stop, I promise I'll be good."

"Bitch shut the fuck up; I'm trying to bust a nut; it's time you give me another kid."

I wouldn't dare give his ass a kid; I got an IUD when I got my 6-week checkup when Harlem was firstborn. I wouldn't be getting pregnant anytime soon. I laid there and endured the torture until Si' finished. He took a shower and left the apartment. I cried myself to sleep. It wasn't always like this; I still remember the first time Si' made love to me, it was so special, and I thought I truly was in love.

***The first time.......***

That night I met Si' we talked for hours on the phone. I found out he was 20 years old. I didn't lie about my age. I told him I was 16 and a senior in high school, my future goals, and my career path. When I say me and him clicked, it was unbelievable to me. There wasn't a day that went by that we weren't together. He lived up the street from me, and I didn't even know it. He would walk me to the bus stop to go to school or work, bring me lunch, and wait for me to get off. He was the best; mind you, this was before I gave him some. But honey, let me tell you when I did give him some, that nigga had a young girl weak, this nigga dick was like a third leg.

The first time we did, it was Election Day (how ironic). We were chilling at my house when the kissing and touching wasn't enough. It had been four months since we met and three months since we became official. I guess Si' was tired of going home with blue balls, and my lil cat wanted to be scratched. Although Si' was grown, I wasn't so he couldn't go past the living room in my house. There we were on my momma's couch watching American Pie when Si' decided he wanted to eat some pie, literally. Si' started rubbing my thighs like he always did when he wanted to fool around; we had been in this same position many times before; it never got past him playing with my pussy and licking my juices off his finger. However, tonight

was different.

"Lay."

"Yea Si.'"

"Let me taste you."

I was so confused and hot, he was stroking my clit with

his middle finger, and that shit was feeling so good.

"Can I Lay, can I taste you?"

"Si', we can't my mom's upstairs."

He didn't hear me or didn't care cause before I knew it,

my titties were in his mouth, first the left one then the right. He

bit down on my nipple, a lil bit that caused pain but felt good at

the same time. Si' put my hand on his dick. I was scared as shit

after I touched it. It was so big. He pulled my shirt over my head

and laid me down on the floor. Si' didn't know this, but I was a

virgin. No one knew it, and I wasn't about to tell him now. He

parted my legs with his knees, made a trail down my body with

his lips; the next thing I felt was his mouth on me. He started off

by licking at first, then biting, then sucking, one finger, two

fingers, biting, and kissing. "Shit Si' that feels good. OMG Si'
don't stop." Oh god. My legs started shaking. I couldn't explain
this feeling, but it felt like heaven on earth. I was cumming all in
Si's mouth, and he just lapped all my juices up.

Si' had me feeling some type of way. Just when I
thought it was over without warning, Si' entered me. I froze; I
was completely in shock. Had he known I was a virgin, I'm sure
he would have been a little gentler with that part. Si' slowly
stroked me, whispering how good I felt and how tight I was. The
more he was able to inch inside of me, the better it started to
feel. After about 45 minutes and a position change, I was a pro,
throwing it back and everything. That night I fell in love with
Si'. But that was years ago. Before the baby, before he cheated
on me (twice that I know about) before he decided I would be
his human punching bag and before I decided enough was
enough.

# Good Girlz With Hood Habits

***Back to the present.......***

      I woke up to my four-year-old standing at the foot of my bed. Harlem was used to the beatings by now, and I hated that he saw me go through this. I wanted him to live in a two-parent home. I was staying so he could have a better living situation than I did. Although I had everything I wanted as a child, I still didn't have my father in my life. I never wanted Harlem to go through that.

"Mommy, we leave; I have eight monies from my birthday you can have if we just leave please, mom."

      I couldn't believe my ears. I never wanted this for my child, and at that point, I knew it was time to get the fuck out of this house and leave Si' for good.

"Baby hold on to your money. We are going to leave, I promise, can you just give mommy about two weeks, then we can go visit God Mommy Eboni, and Uncle Trevor how does that sound?"

 "Okay, mommy, but we got to get out of here, daddy is going to hurt you really bad one day."

# Good Girlz With Hood Habits

He walked out of my room, and I put my plan in motion. Eboni was my best friend that I met while I was in high school. We met at a performance art camp for high schoolers. We instantly clicked even though we lived hundreds of miles apart. She was the only one I knew would help me, and Si' wouldn't fuck with me if I was there because her man didn't play. He was connected with Moshi, who was like God here in Baltimore. I texted Eboni and told her I'd be at her house in two weeks, and I needed a place to stay. Of course, she welcomed me with open arms.

The next day I called off work. I needed to get some shit in order. Si' didn't come home for three days. At that time, I put in my 30 days to vacate my apartment, found an apartment near Eboni and her family, and found a school for Harlem. I got all my mail forwarded to Eboni's house for now and went to the bank and started a new bank account. I tried not to say or do anything that would upset Si'. I had less than two weeks; hopefully, I would never see his face again. If this were one of those urban novels, I would have gotten him killed, and had a clean-up crew on speed dial. But this was my life and I had to do

what was best for my kid and me. Little did I know I was leaving

a monster to lay down with Satan himself.......

# Good Girlz With Hood Habits

Bryan Rollins A.K.A. GM

I've always had to get it out of the mud. My father was a fucking junkie, and my mom worked like a Hebrew fucking slave. Before I tell you about my fucked ass life, let me introduce myself. My name is Bryan Rollins, but everyone calls me GM because I "Get Money." Since I was ten, I have been a hustling lil nigga. I did some fucked up shit in my life for money, and looking back on it; I wouldn't change shit I did. I was all about the dollar. I had bitches falling in love with me just to get what the fuck I wanted. I was fucking these streets up and not giving a damn. Until the day Lalani Williams entered my fucking life. She had my ass open, but I played lil mama so bad. When I first met her, she was still in high school. I caught a bid and didn't see her for years. And when I did, she was in a fucked-up situation with her kid's father. I should have left her the fuck alone; hell, I was married with four kids no one knew about. But Lay was in a position that was crucial and beneficial to me and my empire. So, I made her fall in love with me. Had her breaking laws and fucking her raw. Even had a baby by her ass. If you asked me now, I'd tell you I was really in love with shorty, but my love for money fucked up whatever we could have had together. Let me explain. Here's my story.

**13 years ago……**

June 3, 2007, was the worst day of my fucking life! My brother and I were on our way to this graduation party for my nigga Marty. This little nigga was the only one of us to graduate from high school, so we went all out. We street niggas, so you know we blew money on strippers, liquor, food, weed, X, and everything else, plus we had an all-white theme going. We were dressed to the max. My nigga Diddy had on the all-white Lacoste joint with some fresh air forces and an icy fitted. We let Marty rip Nordstrom's apart, I mean, it was his big day, so it was only right. Let me tell you my lil nigga did it big with the white Burberry short sleeve shirt, the crisp Burberry shorts, and what set this lil dude apart was he didn't even do a sneaker; my man went hard with some butter-soft grown and sexy soft bottoms. Yo shorty was icy, but of course, I had to fuck both their heads

# Good Girlz With Hood Habits

up with my shit. I came down Marty's basement with the all-white True Religion jeans, a True Religion shirt with the red horseshoe, some thin-framed Ray Bands, and the all-white Giuseppe Zanotti tennis. MAN!!!! I was the shit. You hear me. But I had a bigger surprise for my niggas when we got outside.

I traded my 01 Honda coupe for that Dodge Charger. You see, I was getting money and not just play money. I had Northeast Baltimore on lock. I sold crack, dope, weed, pills, pussy you named it, I sold it. I had a one-stop-shop. Every month I was taking home $75,000 in profit alone. And my team was eating well too. I had some of the baddest bitches you could think of. But that shit didn't help me that night. Something told me to stay my black ass at the party; I had been talking to this cute redbone with a gap; she was a little on the thick side, but I was loving her shyness, cute gap, and her hips set out just right. Plus, I could tell lil mama was educated for real. Unlike these termites, I'm used to. Anyway, shorty was telling me about getting into some college; I can't remember that shit now. All I was worried about was fucking and dipping on her cute ass. But shorty wasn't buying my "I got money speech." It seems like she was getting some of her own. Lil mama had on an all-white Adidas sweatsuit that's was tight in all the right places but what fucked my head up was she had on the same tennis I did. Now, these shoes cost a stack, so how the fuck could she afford them? She must have been one of my worker's chick or something.

My nigga Diddy came over to where me and shorty were talking (I heard someone call her Lay, so I guess that was her name) and asked me to go handle something with him. Shorty wasn't trying fuck, so I was like cool, fuck her; I'm out. Why the hell did I do that? This dummy had me riding around West Baltimore for two hours. Looking for what I still to this day do not know. Anyway, long story short, we got pulled over and guess what was under my damn seat, a fucking gun. It took them police bitches all of five minutes to arrest my ass. Shit!

*2011………*

"Rollins, pack up; you're out of here."

# Good Girlz With Hood Habits

That was music to my fucking years. I spent the last four years of my life out Cumberland, Maryland, doing time for a fucking gun I had no intention of using. This shit wasn't supposed to happen to me but fuck it; it's a part of the game, I guess. I went into the joint a, 19-year-old thousandaire with no high school diploma and a rack of expensive clothes I couldn't wear. Man, these last four years really taught me who was on my side and on was just in it for the ride. Let me start off by telling y'all about my wife. That bitch married me to prove a point to her old ass fucking friends. I was 17 when I met Rochelle; she was my next-door neighbor and would flirt with me all the time. One day I stepped to her on some boss shit. It was late on a Friday night, and she was sitting on the steps when I pulled up.

"Yo, Rochelle, what you doing out this time of night?"

"Waiting for your sexy ass."

"Rochelle, stop playing with me like I won't fuck your sexy ass right here on these steps."

# Good Girlz With Hood Habits

"I got a bed and an empty house, no need to fuck on the steps, let me show you how a real woman throws this pussy."

That was all she wrote. Rochelle had me open. She would cook, clean, fuck, and suck me dry. Rochelle was 27 with two kids and had my ass playing stepdad, going to school plays, and basketball games. But Rochelle was insecure and childish. She got pregnant with my twins when I was 18; I ended up marrying her at the courthouse and adopting her two kids. That was the worst fucking thing I could have done. Don't get me wrong; I love all four of my kids, but Rochelle was a sneaky, deadbeat mother.

When I caught my bid, she took all the kids to my mother's and started fucking with my right-hand man. Not to mention, she stole $62,000 from me. The two bitches thought I was going to be gone forever. Jokes on them, and that dumb bitch thought she got over on me when she took that little bit of money from me. Little did she know I got $250,000 stacks in a safe deposit box just waiting for me that nobody knows about.

# Good Girlz With Hood Habits

I did get my GED while I was locked up and took a few cooking classes. That was done to pass the time by. I'm a street nigga; I'm going back out in these streets and get on my grind like I'm used to doing. Fuck that straight and narrow shit. I'd sell sunglasses to a blind man if I had too just to be rocking the latest fashions with a bad bitch on my arms. That's me, and I'm never changing. Fuck it.

I had been out the joint for two weeks, and already I can tell shit wasn't the same. First off, my nigga Marty (the one we had the party for) changed his life around, and instead of going to college as we discussed so at least one of us could be a financial alibi for the team, this nigga was knee-deep in the drug game. I mean, this nigga was the new plug on the streets. Which I'm not mad at, but I can't believe Diddy let this happen. Speaking of Diddy chump ass, this dude got my wife pregnant and then became a fucking pill head. Like what part of the game is that? I know he remembered what Biggie said, "Never get high on your own supply."

# Good Girlz With Hood Habits

I swear when I heard how my nigga fucked the game up, I was hurt. I know I wish that nigga would get control over his bitch, the bitch kept calling my fucking phone with that let's work it out, I thought you were gone forever, I was lonely bull shit. "It cost me a lot, my chain and my watch. They say time is money, but really it's not," J Cole blasted thru my iPhone 3. Speaking of the damn devil, it was Rochelle.

"What yo!"

"Why you answer the phone like that?"

"Why are you calling me? Where your baby daddy at?"

"Come on, GM, we've been thru too much for you to not at least listen to me. I mean, it wasn't like you were faithful the whole time we were together, and nigga you left me out here with nothing. Like what the fuck was I supposed to do? Remember, I was your ride or die, I put hella of shit in my name for you, and fucked and sucked you like crazy. You can't just throw that away."

# Good Girlz With Hood Habits

"Bitch you knew what the fuck it was; you knew thee life I lived. Your ass wanted to be Brandy so fucking bad with your 'I want to be down' head ass."

"Really, GM, what you mad because I fucked Diddy?"

"Bitch you stole from me; this isn't bout you fucking my best friend, where the fuck is my money, Rochelle?"

"Nigga the money is gone, damn you pressed over that petty ass money. What you broke or something?"

"Bitch fuck you."

I hung up on her ass. She must got me fucked up. I didn't have time for Rochelle's ass. I needed to get my team back together. I had to holler at Marty's ass; it was no way I would be working for a nigga that I used to take care of. This nigga was tripping if he thought I was going back on the block. I called my little brother (on my father's side) Twon up and see if he was ready to get back to this money. But I found out he got booked and was given football numbers on some Rico drug charges. Shit, I needed to think, it seems like my whole team was either locked up, smoked out, or worked for Marty. I needed some head and a drink.

I wanted a new starting five of bitches, so I went where bitches always are. The mall out Towson had seriously stepped up in the world. They had bigger and better stores and some fine ass white girls too. Yo, that shit fucked my head up. I was like a kid in the candy store. I got so into shopping, I forgot about looking for new chicks to add to the team. I did see this one chick that I was feeling. I think I knew shorty from somewhere.

"Excuse me, can I talk to you for a minute?"

"Not really."

I knew where I knew her from; it was shorty from the last party I went to; shit, what was her name? Kay? Tay? Lay, it was Lay! Shorty had gained a lil more weight but was still cute as shit with her gap. I sized her up. She was about 5'8, maybe a size 14/16, and long black hair. I couldn't really see her ass because she was wearing some navy-blue uniform pants and rocking Nike boots; she looked like a cop or something from the waist down. Before I could say anything, some tall ass dude came walking up to her with a slick dressed nigga I assumed was their son. He looked like a clown for real, but that wasn't my call to judge the next man. I just walked away from the family. But I heard him say, "Why the fuck was that nigga in your face, is that one of those inmates from your jail that you want to fuck? Wait until I get you to the house; I'm going to fuck you up." When I looked back, I saw past her beauty and saw the sadness in her eyes. Shorty was in a fucked-up situation. Damn!

# Good Girlz With Hood Habits

Lay

The day I saw GM in the mall would forever be the turning point in my life. After the beating Si gave me that night, I changed everything about me. Shit, I was scared to do for years was done in a matter of days. There was only so much a woman could take. I was trying to make this work for Harlem's sake, but Si' never spent time with him or me, and Harlem was starting to hate his father. I always felt like Si' hated Harlem, or maybe it was the relationship Harlem, and I had.

Si' didn't have a relationship with his mother and didn't know his father. I gave Harlem my last name. Fuck, I wasn't married to his ass, and I'm the one that was going to end up taking care of him, so why not? Plus, my dad would have killed me if I didn't give my first child his name. Si' was just an overall dick head. He was four years older than me and thought I was his damn daughter.

# Good Girlz With Hood Habits

## GM

I wish baby girl luck, but that shit wasn't my problem. I moved on with my day like that shit didn't happen. I felt bad for baby girl, but I mind my own business. She did stay on my mind for the rest of the day. Well, that was until I met this bad chick in the food court. I mean shorty was bad! She was rocking some True jeans, with a wife-beater, a cream leather jacket, and some Ugg's with the fur around the top part. Shorty was thick as shit too; her ass was the first thing that greeted me. I thought she could be wifey until she opened her fucking mouth.

Oh my god, this girl could have won hood rat of the year. Everything about her was just extra. I tried to get past her speech or lack of and just see what was in her head. But this bitch must have thought my first name was Bank because all she kept saying was, "Buy me this, pay for that." She was bold; I give her that. I would have even spent a lil bread on ma, but she was too easy.

I bought her food from the burger joint Flamers, ice cream from Cold Stone, and a BeBe sweatsuit, and this chic had my dick in her mouth before we left the parking lot. I busted all in her mouth, then took her to her house and fucked her on the couch. She did have some good pussy, though. That shit was super wet, a little loose, though, but it did the job. I'm so glad I had a condom on me because there's no way I would have gone in her raw dog. When I was done, she wanted to be on some ole cuddling, hold me shit. I had to let baby girl know I wasn't the relationship type, but like all women, she hit me with that. "You just don't know a good woman when you see one." She's kidding me, right? I wanted to say, "What your sister upstairs because your hoe ass ain't got nothing good on you but your head game." Instead, I just hit her with the, "Look shorty; I'm out, here's my number; text me later."

I got the fuck out of there real fast. This bitch was geeking if she thought I was wifing her hoe ass. Ladies, please tell me why in the hell would I even entertain the thought of having a serious relationship with someone who didn't know my last name before she knew what my cum tasted like? I couldn't dwell on that simple bitch. I had to get up with Marty about getting back to the money. I mean, after replenishing my clothes and getting me a lil crib by the water, my money was running low. I probably should have chilled on spinning, but that's just not in my DNA, you feel me.

So, I took 50 stacks and got me a 3-bedroom, 3.5-bathroom condo overlooking the water, my rent was $3200 a month flat, but I paid it up for a year. I had to pay a lil extra so they wouldn't inquire about my financial situation. I gave the leasing manager an extra two stacks plus my number, and all the paperwork was taking care of. Lol! I swear the power of dick and money is priceless. I took what was left over from the 50k and hit every furniture store in the DMV. I was a street nigga, but I had taste. My shit was laid. My color pattern was black and white.

I got some hot shit, and my man 100grand (that's his name) hooked me up with his Wal-Mart plug, so I had 64 inch TV's in my living room and bedroom, a 42 inch in the guest room, surround sound, iPods, laptops, iPads, and not to mention lil shorty that I fucked from the mall worked at IKEA, so she hooked me up with decorative things for the crib. Once all that was out the way, I had to get me some new wheels. I still had the charger, but it was in snake ass Rochelle's name, so I knew what would come with trying to get that back, plus she needed it for her big-headed ass baby anyway.

Oh, my kids were living with my mother down in PG County. My mother went and got custody of the two oldest kids. Since she wasn't blood-related, a lot of stuff she couldn't do it without the papers. Rochelle didn't give a damn. The kids would come over to my place every weekend. They all had their own room at my mom's house, but the boys shared a room at mine, and the girls shared the other room at my home. I copped a 2011 Chevrolet Camaro Convertible. This baby had 312-hp and a V6 engine. I could have gotten the limited edition, but that shit sold out in 3 minutes. But it's cool; this only set me back 30k. With the apartment clothes, shoes, and whip, my 250k was down to $162,500. I copped a Jeep Wrangler to drive when I had the kids. I needed to get my hands on some work and a profitable block.

# Good Girlz With Hood Habits

"Yo!"

"Marty, my nigga, its GM. I'm hungry."

"Oh, yeah, my nigga, well, I just hit the store; we got mad food in the house what you trying to eat."

"Mannnn, I'm starving. I'm trying to get some of that chicken you be making; I heard that shit be hitting."

"Say no more. I'm in the kitchen now, how many wings do you want?"

"My G, I'm starving, so fix me like ten or better."

"Damn my nigga you are starving! But cool, come thru white girl crib, and I got you."

"I'm on my way, oh yeah I need some lemonade, and skittles too."

"Say no more. One!"

That's the shit I'm talking about. I just ordered a key of the rawest coke, some crack, and some pills. My shit was about to be popping. I counted out 25k from my stash and put the rest away. I had a meeting with the bank in the morning to put some dollars in the stock market. I'm a hood nigga, but I'm not stupid either. I got to have something else going on other than drugs.

Me and Marty hooked up, and I got dirt cheap prices too. I paid 13.5 for the key, seven stacks for the crack, and yo gave me the pills; he said niggas was starting to fuck with something called buks, so the need for pills wasn't that high. Shitttting me, I bet I make these bitches sell. Anyway, after handling business, I felt like doing something. I wanted to go out, but my "bitch roster" wasn't really up. The leasing manager had a husband, so I could only deal with her during her business hours, and there wasn't a way in hell I was calling Rochelle snake ass, so I had to hit up the hood rat.

I ended up taking her to the movies, and some new fast-food Mexican joint called Chipotle. I guess the four years I was away bitches' standards lowered. Fuck it a date that would have cost me $100-$150 only ran me $52.33. I didn't even want to fuck, so I took her home and went home myself. I had an early day in the morning and needed to rest if I was going take the streets over again.

# Good Girlz With Hood Habits

Lay

While with Si' I lived in a 3-bedroom, 3bath condo, driving a 2009 BMW and a 2008 Honda Accord. Everyone thought I lived a perfect life, but little did they know I was living in hell. What Si' didn't know was, I was getting promoted. I got the letter a few days before the fight and never got around to telling him about it. I was finally becoming a SGT. I had to wait until I was weapons qualified and 21, although I worked there for two years before my 21$^{st}$ birthday.

I lucked up and found a 2-bedroom condo that was move-in ready. Eboni wanted me to stay longer, but her house was already crowded, and I didn't want to impose any more than I had too. The place reminded me of the place I stayed at now, but it was much cheaper. I decided I was going to leave and not tell Si' so I needed all new everything. I had a little less than six thousand dollars in my savings account and a total of $7,500 on my three credit cards. My 21$^{st}$ birthday was in two months, and my dad's lawyer already contacted me to come to sign and get my check. I thought my trust fund was something small, maybe $10-$15k, but I soon found out I was about to

become a millionaire. But I'll save that for later. Right now, let's

get back to all the changes Harlem and I are going through.

I left the apartment I shared with Si' with only an

overnight bag. We had clothes at Eboni's house already, and she

went and brought Harlem a shitload of things that he probably

didn't need. I even left the car I got Si' for his 25th birthday. He

was going have to use that car as shelter after they put his ass

out because clearly, he wasn't going be able to afford $2,200 in

rent alone with his no job having ass. In the spirit of "out with

the old," I went to the BMW dealer to see what I could get on

my trade-in. My car was only two years old; it only had 32000

miles because I was never allowed to go anywhere. The dealer

showed me three different cars, another BMW, a Jag, and a

Volkswagen Jetta. I choose the Jetta. I needed to downsize since

I now had to pay for childcare for my son. It was April 13, 2011,

a Monday that I took back over my damn life.

I moved into my fully furnished home on April 28, 2011,

with a new crib, a new car, and a new job. I was sure my life was going to be much better. Never would I've imagined my new life

would have consisted of drug, sex, and criminal citations.........

# Good Girlz With Hood Habits

It had been a month since I got my team together. I had a small group of six goons, young bulls ready to make this money. We got back on the grind on my same block. Marty and I came to an understanding. I would keep this block with him being my plug, and I'd buy two bricks a month at 15.5. My first week was rough, man. I had to get my clients back up, but by me not knowing how to cook my shit, I had to rely on Marty to cook it, and he stepped on it way too much. I told him about his fat ass; he knew what the fuck he was doing. Going tell me because of the price I was paying, blah blah blah some shit I didn't want to hear, so I gave him an extra $3,500 to just give me my shit raw.

Now I had the entire product and didn't know the first thing about cooking that shit. Fuck! Man, this drug dealing shit was starting to become stressful. For days I was sitting on raw coke. I was chilling in my crib watching a funny lil nigga on YouTube name Gsongz; that nigga was the next Kevin Hart, I swear. Then it hit me, "GM Google that shit." It's amazing what you can find on Google. I learned how to cook that shit myself and make a homemade bomb. Yo, what the fuck is this world coming too? With only cutting my shit once, my client list shot through the roof. Within two weeks, I had my block doing numbers again. I had to get Marty to up my order to four bricks a month.

I had this one young bull on my team named BJ; his brother used to be my right-hand man before I got knocked, I heard he was throwing bricks at the jail. But peep this shit out, the nigga was making fucking money behind those walls, and I'm not talking about that bull shit as state money. I mean, this nigga was sending home 15 racks a week. Isn't that some shit? I told BJ to tell his brother to put me on his visiting list. I needed to know how this nigga was making money on the inside and how I could be down.

In the meantime, I had put my team on. We were seeing 100k a week in profit alone. My bad bitch roster was back up. I had the leasing manager, the hood rat, a stripper bitch, and a dentist on my daily rotation. Although that chick

# Good Girlz With Hood Habits

Lay stayed on my mind, I was good with the bitches I had. I even let Rochelle come suck my dick from time to time. The old bitch head game couldn't be fucked with. Yeah, I let that bitch taste the god every once in a while. Shit, she could put super head out business. Life was good again. No one could have ever told me shit would change in a matter of minutes.

Ever since 2007, I haven't done parties, I'm sure you can see why. But anyway, one of my soldiers was turning 21, and niggas wanted to hit the club. Something in my head told me to stay my ass home, don't go. But nooo, I wanted to see some bitches. Worst mistake I've ever made in my life! You know I'm all about the money, so when Lil BJ hit me up to bring some Molly's with me to the club cause some white bitches wanted to let loose, I was all for it. Why the fuck did I take the Camaro out, and why the fuck would I carry 35 Molly's with me and why the fuck was I going to that dumb ass party? A question I asked myself as I was being booked and charged with possession to distribute a controlled substance.

# Good Girlz With Hood Habits

Lay

***Three months* later.......**

I don't know why I took this promotion; I was better staying where I was. I thought becoming a SGT would make my workload a little less stressful and enjoyable but not here in the city. Oh no, down here, a SGT is just a damn title. I still work sections, but now I have to do paperwork, reports, rounds for the entire jail, deal with disgruntled inmates, CO's, and power-tripping supervisors. So not worth the extra 6% pay increase. They could have kept that. Today I was working a section because, of course, we were short-staffed like always. Anyway, they had me on G-section, a section in the Southside of the jail that housed 94 inmates waiting to be sentenced, convicted, or released. This whole floor was called "indictment row" because either you were indicted from outside criminal activities or on your way to being indicted from the shit that was going on, on the inside. I hated this shit.

Every time I worked here, I was reminded of who was supposed to be out and not in a nice way. This side of the jail was "run" by BGF (Black Gorilla Family); they controlled the sex

and drugs that entered the institution. My first day in this

section, a co-worker came up to me and said, "Don't be dumb;

let the brothers out." Me being the square I was, I was like, "I'm

not letting all the black guys out and leave the other races

locked in, that's rude." I swear this girl must have thought I was

the dumbest person in the world. Shit, I didn't know what she

was talking about. My brothers weren't locked up here, so what

other brothers were she talking about? Well, come to find out

that's what the "organization" (because they don't call

themselves a gang) referred to each other as "brothers." After

she explained that to me, I was scared as shit. It was like 25

"brothers" in that section alone. I wasn't letting all these people

out of their cells for no apparent reason. So, no one came out.

No working men, food cart workers, nobody! Hell, I didn't want

to let the guys that had to go on medical passes out of the cell.

Around 1200 hours, the guy that slept in the first cell

called my name. When I got to the cell, I was surprised to see it

was that guy from Marty's graduation party. I never knew his name, but there he was sitting on my section looking sexy as shit.

"Yo, what's up why none of the working men out?"

"It's nothing to be done; it's no need for them to be out."

"Look shorty if you are trying to have a good day, I advise you to pop some of these coochies and let us out."

Popping coochies mean open the grills, don't worry, I didn't know what it meant at first either.

"Listen, I'm not opening anything until need be."

"Who the fuck you talking too, do you know who I'm? I run this section, you better call your SGT, rookie and find out what the fuck is going on around here."

"Let me tell you something, I run this section, and I'm the SGT on duty, and if I say no grills are being open, then that's what I mean you better ask about me."

And with that, I walked away. Not 10 minutes later, a LT came walking up to me.

"Sgt. Williams, why are all the grills locked?"

"Isn't it MSC, (MSC is code for total lockdown in the jail) why would they be open?"

"I don't know how your used to doing things but down here, we like to keep things quiet, let the working men out, and don't cause any problems for us."

I was fucking confused at this point like I was doing what I was supposed to, and I still got in trouble. I didn't like how this lady was talking to me and why the fuck should I let people out when clearly there's no need for them to be out?

"Lt. Charles, I'm a little confused, but MSC is MSC, and no one is supposed to be out, so you can take you and your attitude off my section because unlike most of the people working here, I'm not scared of these dudes nor am I scared of you for that matter."

"Let me tell your green ass something, these niggas here run this jail, not your high yellow ass. They keep shit in order and make it so you can go home at 3 pm, so don't fuck up our shit with your topflight security ass. Get with the program, and you might end up with a few dollars and a new man. So, let the

fucking working men out and chill out, shit."

Oh, I know this shit wasn't happening to me; this bitch

had me fucked up. Now I'm not sure when or where my so-

called courage came from, but I'm glad that shit kicked in

because three months ago, I would have taken her bull shit and

said nothing but those days were the fuck over. So, while she

thought she was about to walk away, I kindly handed her the

keys and j-unit (the J-unit is what we call the sections walkie-

talkie) to this funky ass section and walked off! Fuck this place;

I'm out!

Now, this is where shit got worse. I went to the so-

called Chief of Security office to explain to her what happened

and to write a formal complaint, but I sure was in for a damn

surprise. Maybe I should have knocked first, but I was just so

hyped and mad that I just walked right in. Well, to my surprise,

my Chief of Security was ummmm, for lack of better words, a

little busy. There she was on all fours with her black pencil BeBe

skirt pulled up, getting fucked like a dog. Now I'm all for the work hump romance with your dude, but this nigga wasn't her husband. Judging from the green pants and shirt, he was an inmate.

"Oh, yes, fuck me, go deeper."

"You like this shit, don't you?"

"Yes, yes, yes, oh my god."

"Shut up bitch, did I say you could talk?" (smack)

"Oh, shit, I'm sorry, daddy."

"Bitch didn't I tell you to shut up, turn over, suck my dick since you want to talk so much, talk on this dick."

And with that, she turned around and sucked all her own juices off his penis. Now she never saw me, but he did; he stared me right in my eyes and placed a finger up to his lips as if to say "hush" and winked his eye. OMG, what the fuck have I gotten myself into? I backed out of the office. I couldn't take this place anymore. I went to the duty captain and told them I was leaving early. I felt sick. What type of place is this? I had heard of officers fucking inmates, but I never saw that shit with my own eyes. I took off for three days after that. I was scared to go back, like what else was going to happen.

Ring, ring, ring

My house phone rang, which was weird because I never used it. Matter fact, only people that knew the number was my job and my doctor's office.

"Hello!"

"Can I speak to Lay?"

"This is she, who is this?"

"Let's just say I'm an old friend."

"Who is this before I hang up this damn phone!"

"Hold up, ma, first off, watch that damn mouth, second you ain't hanging up on the love of your life."

"Okay, who the fuck is this, and you better give me a name before I fucking hang up now?"

"Damn bae, it's GM."

"GM, who, I don't know, no damn GM."

"Yea, you do. Think about it, and I'll call you later, my love."

With that, the caller hung up. That was so fucking strange to me. I couldn't even call back because the number was blocked. I didn't let that shit take too much of my time; I had my own fucking issues to deal with.

Issue #1 My Baby Daddy

By this time, me and Si' had been apart for about three months. He didn't know my new number, where I lived, or where I was working. I didn't even tell my mom any of that information because I knew she would tell him so imagine my surprise when I get a message on Facebook from, Si'TheDon.

Si'TheDon: Bitch where are you and my fucking son.

Rude_Girl: FUCK YOU!

Si'TheDon: I swear on everything I love when I find you, I'm killing you.

Rude_Girl: WON'T YOU TELL THAT BITCH BEE-BEE TO KILL THAT BASTARD ASS BABY OF YOURS.

Si'TheDon: OH, YOU GOT BALLS NOW. LAY STOP PLAYING WITH ME. YOU KNOW YOU ONLY HURTING YOURSELF IN

THE LONG RUN. YOU MY BITCH ALWAYS AND FOREVER.

I'M FORGET THIS LIL DISAPPEARING ACT AND LET YOU

COME GET ME FROM MIKEY CRIB WITHOUT ME KICKING

YOUR ASS, BUT THIS OFFER WON'T LAST FOREVER.

This man must have lost his damn mind, and after that message, I deleted my damn account. Fuck him and that social network. I'll stick with IG.

Issue #2: My Job

I couldn't stay away for too long. So, Monday morning, I walked back in that jail with a fucked-up attitude. And I will be damn if they didn't put me back on fucking G-section. I was over this shit already. These fucking inmates and dirty ass officers were causing my blood pressure to skyrocket. Here I was walking down the fucking tier doing my count, and I hear all types of degrading shit from these fluke ass dude. Ugh, I think it's time for a new career change. The last cell I get to is the one and only asshole from the other day.

# Good Girlz With Hood Habits

"Take the sheets of your grill sir, and get ready to come out to feed up the section."

"Oh, snap, I thought you had quit woman, but I see you're getting with the program around here."

"Sir, remove the sheets from the grill and get ready for work."

This nigga was a fucking thorn in my side. He thought he was so fucking cute and was the HNIC on this section, shitttttt!

"Yo hit cell 1 /2 on the east bottom and 59/60 on the west bottom."

"I'm not."

"What? Why?"

"Sir, you and your cell body are the only two coming out right now."

He laughed and said, "Ard, Lay damn, you do what you want, don't you?"

Wait pause, how did he know my damn name?

"Oh, don't look like that, I know a few things about you, Miss Laylania Williams, and next time your future husband calls, you better be nice."

# Good Girlz With Hood Habits

And with that, he walked away. OMG, he was the one that called me. But how did he get my number? What did he want from me? Should I report this? Hell no! Knowing these fucked up people, they're probably the ones that gave him my number in the first place. Anyway, the rest of the day went by pretty uneventful, no codes, no reports to write. I went home, and me and HC had a mommy and son day that consisted of shopping, eating, and watching the movie Car's. Around 10:30, I got another mysterious call.

"Listen, I know you know who this is, right?"

"Yes, I am aware."

"Oooohhh, no smart mouth tonight, huh?"

"You might want to state your reason for calling me before I hang up."

The truth of the matter, I wasn't going to hang-up. For some reason, I wanted to talk to him, besides, the whole, "I run this jail thing," he seemed cool. Needless to say, I stayed on the phone all night. We talked about everything under the sun, from his failed relationship with his baby mother, his father, and to what happened to him that night at Marty's party. It didn't hit me until he put me on hold because the "police" was at his grill that I was talking to an inmate on an illegal cell phone for hours. I ended the conversation right there and told him as much as I was feeling him; this could never happen again. I hung up and called Comcast to have the phone service removed immediately. Wow, the best conversation I've had in a long time with the opposite sex was from an inmate. I shook my head and went to sleep, mentally preparing for what work would bring in the morning.

When I got to work, to my surprise Mr. Rollins didn't say too much to me, which caught me by surprise, and I was a little salty. Nevertheless, I kept it moving with my day, and by the end of the week, I had almost forgotten all about our 3-hour conversation. I can't lie though; I was pissed that he didn't try to press up on me. Like I know, I told him not to call again but damn was it that easy to just stop fucking with me. Damn! I couldn't dwell on that anyway. It wasn't like I could deal with his ass. So, for the next month, we never said anything outside of work-related issues. I still kept the section tight, but here and there, I would loosen up some and let like four working men out and or give extra time for the guys' rec time.

Work was coming along okay; I had even made a few friends (in time, I will find out them bitches were not my friends). Shit was cool, except every Friday, I would get this strange envelope with a 14-digit number written on a piece of paper in my mailbox. I didn't know what it was because it wasn't a phone number, and the numbers were always different, and on the back of the envelope would be another 3-digit number. One Friday, I decided to have drinks and crabs over my house with my newfound "friends." It was my girls Chrissie, Mira, and Canny from outside the jail and the girl Barney from the jail coming through to sip and sit.

Barney was 12 years older than me but acted like she was three years younger for real, but she was mad cool and stayed cussing somebody out at the job. The crazy thing is she was the girl who told me to let all the "brothers" out when I first came to BCDC. Anyway, she came over early to help me set up. I guess since we were cool, she felt it was cool to be nosy all on my damn coffee table going through my mail.

"Girl, what are you doing with Green Dot numbers? I knew your ass wasn't as uptight as you seemed, which one you fucking girl?"

"What? What's a Green Dot? Fucking who? Bee, what are you talking about?"

She looked at me like I was a fucking retarded monkey.

"Lay, you don't know what those are? For real? How did you get them?"

"Every Friday, it's a new one in my mailbox."

"Girl, how many do you have?"

"About 8, 9, maybe 10."

"Are you kidding me, and you're not fucking anybody at the jail?"

"Well!"

"I knew it! Who is he bitch? Where he sleep at? Is he a brother?"

# Good Girlz With Hood Habits

"Well, we haven't fucked yet, but I've been talking to Ofc. Jackson, for about three weeks, I think he lives over west, and yeah, he's black. He's on the tact team."

"Really, are you fucking kidding me, Lay, you can't be that green, are you? I'm not talking about a fucking officer; them bitches don't have enough money to pay for this pussy. I mean an inmate Lay. That's who's been sending you these numbers. It's like their way of sending flowers."

"WHAT??? What the fuck does that mean? You know how to use these things?"

"Yeah, the 14-digit number is the number you load on a prepaid card, and this 3-digit number is the amount....... Bitch this say $300, and you got how many? Where are the rest of them at?"

I walked into my bedroom to get the rest. If what Barney was saying was right, I was sitting on a few grand and didn't even know it. Let's see, I had nine Green Dot numbers in total, and each one was $300 or better. Damn, you won't believe this, but one was $900. This shit was crazy; in total, I had $3,800 that I had no idea why I was given them, but I did have an idea of who sent them. I was scared as shit to have that in

my home. I was going to give them to Barney, but then I

thought better of that idea. Instead, I took them all out of the

different envelopes and made it look like I shredded them in my

home office in front of Barney; she is cool, but I don't know, nor

do I trust that bitch. Plus, after all the niggas she told me she

fucked with, I didn't need her to try fuck with GM because of

the money. Nah, that hood rich nigga was going to be mine.

OMG, I can't believe I just claimed him. Lol wow. I couldn't wait

to get back to work now.


***The next day.........***

Of course, I was on G-section the next day, and that was

just what I wanted. I had to show this lil dude that his money

wasn't going to impress me. I had money before this CO job; I

was always on my grind. I stayed with a job, so I didn't need his

money. Niggas always want to throw their money around but

get mad when a chick only wants them for their money.

Although the cash GM sent my way was double my check and

could have been used well at the nearest mall, I was giving it

back, he wasn't getting me that fucking easy. Nah, he was

getting that money back!

"Listen, I don't know how you got all my personal info but stop

calling me, sending stuff to my house, and just leave me alone."

"Ms. Williams, I don't know what you're talking about."

"Yeah, whatever, just don't send this shit to my house anymore.

This little bit of change isn't gonna get you anywhere, that ain't

even half my salary."

Okay, so I was lying, but he didn't know that. All he

needed to know was I wasn't just going to be bought and not

with no petty ass $3,800. After we had that conversation,

neither of us said anything to one another all day or the rest of

the week. I guess he was mad that I gave him the damn

numbers back, but I wasn't losing my job for some petty ass

money.

Well, Friday came back around, and I wondered if I

would get another envelope, but to my surprise and dismay, I

didn't get one. Around 7 pm that night, the front desk called upstairs and said I had a delivery. Well, it's about damn time, I

thought. I had ordered HC some things from the Ralph Lauren

store and Baby Gap that hadn't gotten here yet. Imagine my

surprise when I get downstairs and find two small boxes. First, I

thought maybe all of my items weren't shipped, but when I got

home and opened the boxes, I found a white iPhone 4s, and the

other boxes contained nothing but hundreds. Before I could

count the money or actually get the phone out the box, I heard

a chime-like sound. After further investigation, I realized it was

a text message. That read:

"Look woman, kill all that I'm an independent woman, and I

don't need no man bull shit. I know I'm locked up right now, but

I swear it's only temporary. You know you want me, and I damn

sure want you. Take these ten stacks and blow on you and my

future stepson. I heard his middle name was Bryan, damn that's

destiny right there! I'll make you love me woman. This phone is

just for me. I'll hit you later."

~Your future

# Good Girlz With Hood Habits

## GM

I was fucking speechless; I mean, this nigga was pulling all the stops, ten thousand dollars, and an iPhone? What the fuck was I supposed to do after that? I tell you one thing; I wasn't giving this money back. Fuck that, my son and I were going on vacation as soon as I could get the days off. Damn, I can't lie; this nigga had me open a little bit. Remember, I had been paying all the bills by myself for a long time. And here this dude was just throwing money at me. Well, if it was me he wanted, it was me he was going to get. Just as long as he kept breaking a sister off with money like this. Yeah, I was definitely seeing things GM's way.

# Good Girlz With Hood Habits

## GM

Yeah, I tricked off a little on Lay, but I needed her on my team to take over this jail. She was smart and pretty but not my type for real, but she would do for now. I had to get her to open up about a relationship with me. She was so green to this jail shit; I felt kind of sad for the shit I was about to put her through. But fuck it, I was all about my cash. Them fucking pigs took me off the street in my prime again, but I wasn't going be down forever and trust me, when I hit those streets again, I was going to be the same money getting flashy nigga I was.

I gave Lay a gift every day for two weeks, I texted her from the jimmy mack, and I let my tier know she was my girl. I had her eating that shit out the palm of my hands. On the 15th day of my gift-giving, I asked her to bring me a chicken box. I had to start her off with something easy to see what she would and wouldn't do. First, it was food, then clothes, and within a month time, I had her bringing in pills under her tongue. I kept hitting her with that, "We a team. How I know you can hold me down if you won't help build me up?" I could tell she never really fucked with a nigga on my caliber because shorty believed everything I said. I even got her pregnant once. Oh, what you thought I wasn't going to hit that. Yes, I did, and no lie, Lay pussy was like crack; that's how I ended up falling for her ass. Yeah, yeah, yeah, I know I wasn't supposed to, but baby girl was everything a man could ask for, smart, loyal, submissive, and had a tight wet pussy; the only thing was she didn't give head. I can't live without that shit.

I never told Lay about my kids or my wife. Truth be told, I wasn't supposed to go this far with her. I needed a square to mold so I could take over this jail. My nigga Red Nose had four baby mommas and a whole team of bitches working for him. That nigga was sending 15 stacks home a week after taking care of the guards, his women, and the rest of his team. This nigga was even fucking the Chief of Security. When I say he had this shit on lock, I truly mean that shit. I wasn't hating, but I damn sure wasn't about to be working for the next nigga. So, I had to get my own team. Lay was cool with this other CO that was down for whatever long as the price was right. I hooked up with her a few times, shorty pussy was trash, but her head game was fire. I had Lay put her on our little two-man team, and shit really got moving. Lay was smart as shit but slow with doing what I wanted. So, where she dropped the ball Ofc. Barney would pick up the slack. Barney was trying to take Lay's spot, but that shit wasn't happening. Niggas on the tier called me "Gold's" because my little operation turned into gold within a matter of weeks. Yeah, I was a hot commodity; in other words, I was that nigga for real. However, after doing this shit for six months, I was tired of this childish money and wanted more!

At the time, I was only sending $7500 uptown to mom dukes after paying all the guards, blue shirts, and spoiling Lay ass. I needed more money, so I set it up for Lay's next package from my connect Bobbie to be 4oz of loud, 250 buk strips, a quarter of coke, and $3500 in cash. I knew I was pushing it, but I needed to put my foot down on Lay and let her cute ass know who was running this show.

# Good Girlz With Hood Habits

Lay

Within six months, my whole life changed. I went from not knowing anything to being a part of one of the biggest drug operations to date. My mediocre way of living was changed in the blink of an eye. The Forever 21 clothes and Betsey Johnson bags got switched to True Religion on everything and Gucci bags. I even had a Celine bag in the closet. My cute little comfortable condo got a full makeover, including new floors, bigger TV's, grander bedroom sets, and a maid that came every Tuesday and Thursday. I was getting money from my full-time employment and my man, Mr. GM. I loved that man through the depth of my soul. There wasn't anything anyone could tell me bad about him. In my eyesight, he was The King, I The Queen, and Harlem was our Prince. We were building an empire together, and that made me love him more. He didn't want nor need my money. He gave unselfishly and rarely asked for anything in return. Maybe a plate of food here and there or some pills but never nothing too heavy. He paid my bills, and when we could, he sexed me crazy. Speaking of the devil here,

he is calling me.

"Hey, bae!"

"Woman, what the fuck took you so long to answer the phone?"

"Who the fuck you talking too?"

"Sike bae, what your big head ass doing? Where is my son?"

"Whatever ugly, I'm at the mall, and he's in school."

"You stay at the damn mall spending all my money," he

laughed.

"And you stay getting on my nerves. What do you want, man?"

"What I tell you about that 'man' shit? Look, pick me up

something from Lacoste. I need some shorts; it's hot as hell in

this bitch at night."

"And I'm the one spoiled. Ard bae, you need anything else?"

"Yeah, some head. Hahaha, sike bae, but ummm yeah, can you

pick something up from Bobbie? It's all ready for you."

"Sure, bae, what is it some more buks?"

# Good Girlz With Hood Habits

"Yeah bae, that's it. Ard, I got to go, they are doing a search today, so I'm sending the phone up. I'll hit you late at night. Love you big head."

"Okay, bae. Love you more."

Bobbie was GM's supplier; he sold weed, Molly's, buks, perks, I think he even sold pussy. He was a one-stop-shop type of dude. Anyway, I really hated going to see him; I hated bringing shit in the jail no matter how small it was. It was like my loyalty was being split between the man I loved and my career.

"Hey Bobbie, it's Ty, I'm coming to pick something up for GM."

I never told any of the people I was meeting for GM my real name; I always wore shades or pulled my hat down real low. I was always told never to trust a criminal, and at any given time, GM or anyone else from the "crew" could snitch on my ass. I was "Green" about drugs, but I damn sure wasn't stupid about the law.

"Sure, baby girl, you know where I'm at."

"Over by White Ave, right?"

# Good Girlz With Hood Habits

"Yeah, just meet me at the McDonalds."

"Okay, see you in about 30 minutes."

Bobbie was an old-timer but was like an uncle to GM. When I lost our baby, it was Bobbie that made sure I was okay and brought me some food and stuff. PAUSE! You can take that judgmental look off your damn face. Yes, I fucked an inmate, but he was my nigga; I would do anything for him, so when the love of my life asked for some pussy, I gave it to him. He paid the bills, and as his woman, I had to make sure he felt like the king in our castle... Even if he didn't reside there. I mean, that's what a woman supposed to do, right?

I picked up the package from Bobbie, stopped at Mo's to pick up dinner, got my little man, and went home. I had to get things in order for the next day; you know, iron uniforms, showers, homework, oh, and pack up 300 pills and 250 buk strips, you know the normal shit. Well, at least that's my typical night. I waited for HC to go to sleep before I started my "part-time" job. But when I opened the bag, I was confused as shit. Maybe Bobbie gave me the wrong order.

# Good Girlz With Hood Habits

"Hey Bobbie, this Ty umm, I think you gave me the wrong order."

"Nah, shorty GM said to give you that, I thought you knew he changed the order."

"Oh, umm yeah, I'm tripping my bad. Talk to you later."

I hung up. I didn't want him to know I was completely fucking lost to what was going on. I called GM, and his ass didn't answer. Maybe I was supposed to take it to somebody else. Yeah, that had to be it. There's no way GM was trying to get me to bring all this shit in; it was weed and what I guess to be coke. Yeah, I would wait till he called me to explain what was going on.

*5:30 am the next day.......*

GM never called me back, but the nigga sent a text at 3:07 am talking about, "Bae I love you; remember we a team; you can do this, make daddy proud." What the fuck was that? When I called his ass, he didn't answer but going text me back talking about he feeding the tier; oh, he has lost his fucking mind! Now don't get me wrong, I'm his ride or die, but I'm also HC bread and butter, his mother, his provider. That shit he wanted me to bring in would have given me life with no shot of sunlight ever. No fuck that! I left all that shit in my house and went to work. I didn't take the pills or even his food, not until he explained some shit, his spoiled ass was cut off of everything.

*Three weeks later.......*

I talked all that big shit but guess who was sneaking on GM's section ready to drown his ass in my pussy juices. I picked up overtime on C-shift whenever GM and I wanted to get it in. The officer that worked his tier overnight always fell asleep around 3 am, so that was when I would sneak through the ODR and up the back steps to get to GM's section. He slept on the bottom right side of the tier in the first cell. When I was going down to his cell, I saw another officer sneaking off the next section over, but that's none of my business. Making my way to his cell, this nigga was sitting up doing push-ups looking good as fuck.

# Good Girlz With Hood Habits

"I hope you plan on working me out like that."

"Damn, woman, what took your ass so long to get up here?"

"I was on WDC side, so I had to go through the post 11, through the back door by K-section, walk up them steps then through the ODR."

"You did all that to get this dick; let me find out you miss me."

"You know I do, come bae we only got like twenty minutes."

"Lay, you can't be loud either; we almost got caught last time."

"Bae, you be hitting my spot, give me a sheet, and it better be clean."

"I got you, woman, come here and sit on my face. I need to taste that sweet ass pussy."

I walked in the cell and took my right leg out of my uniform pants, and stood over GM while he was sitting on his blanket on the floor. He didn't have to worry about any panties because I didn't have any on. I knew what I came in for. GM parted my lips and began devouring my pussy; he started out slow, taking his full wide lounge from the front of my pussy to damn near the crack of my ass. Moaning softly, I knew we were going to pass that twenty-minute deadline, but at this point, I

didn't give two fucks. When he stuck that tongue inside of me

and started fucking me with it, I damn near cried. GM knew

what the fuck to do when it came to eating pussy. He slurped,

licked, sucked, and fucked me silly with his tongue. After I came

three times, I was ready to tap out. However, he had other

plans; pushing me on his bunk, GM entered me from the back,

and I damn near lost it. My back was arched in the perfect way

for him to get all up in my guts. This jail sex was cool, but I

needed this man in a bed bigger than my son's twin size bed so

he could fuck me how I've always wanted to be fucked. I'm a

closet freak, and I want whips, choking, handcuffs, all that shit.

GM was going crazy in the pussy, but I needed him to hurry up

so I could get back to my post.

"Damn bae this pussy so fucking good, you better not give this

pussy to any of these fuck boys, I swear this shit don't make no

sense."

"Bae, you feel so good, but we got to hurry up before we get

jammed up."

# Good Girlz With Hood Habits

When I said that, GM went harder and started pulling my hair just like I like it. I squeezed my pussy muscle's and started throwing it back; when I did that, GM made a noise I never heard. This nigga growled like he was a damn dog. Kind of turned me on but scared me too. He came all in me, then got up and went to his sink and got one of the wash rags I brought in to keep for times like this along with a bar of Dove soap and cleaned me up. I rushed to get my clothes on and shot back through the jail to get back to my post. When I got there, my partner was knocked out. I slipped down the hall to my dorm and silently thanked the Lord for getting me through this shit.

I know I'm risking it all, and I could lose my job, but damn that shit was fun. As much fun as it was fucking GM in his cell, I hated what came with dealing with him. For example, here I am on a Friday night trying to figure out how to pack 16oz of weed in my panties for the third time this week. I can't believe how shit changed in a matter of weeks. The kind, loving, gift-giving man I fell in love with turned into my money-hungry, sex addict boss! Every sweet convo we had turned into bring this up here, drop this off there, flip this money, and don't spend that money. The calls, text, and special kites were replaced with orders and demands. The only good thing that was left was the sex. This nigga ate my pussy like I was the last supper. GM fucked me in more ways than one.

I found out he had a wife and four kids that he never told me about, and I'm not 100%, sure but I think he was fucking Barney on the low. As good as he changed my life financially, he destroyed my career and my self-esteem. But for some strange reason, I couldn't leave his ass. Little did I know I would be leaving him sooner than later on a one-way ticket to prison. Something told me to call out that day or at least leave some of that shit home. My momma always told me to go with my first instinct. But I didn't listen.

Usually, when you walk into the employee side of the jail, you walk through a security scanner, get a simple pat-down, and go about your business. However, today they did what you call a "detailed search," which included a damn dog! To tell you I was scared shitless would be an understatement!

# Good Girlz With Hood Habits

Okay, Lay calm down, calm down, you can do this. It's packed tightly, and you have the dryer sheets around it, they won't smell anything. Man fuck this shit. When I got to the door, I pretended I left my ID in my car, so that I could get back to the parking lot. I tell you, I couldn't get that shit off of me fast enough. Thank God I had tents on my car. I pulled that shit off me so fast and hard; I know I pulled some of my pussy hairs but ask me did I give a damn? No, I was over my ride or die for GM's ass phase; that shit was too close to comfort. Soon as I got to him, I was going tell him to fuck off; I wasn't losing my freedom for anybody. Over it.com

# Good Girlz With Hood Habits

## GM

Mann, when I tell you I fucked up with Lay, that shit is unbelievable. My shorty saw that package and flipped on my ass. She stopped taking my calls, turned the iPhone off, and refused to work my section. To be honest with you, I was sick. As much as I don't want to admit it, Lay had my heart; I just couldn't be with her. This shit was only temporary. We lived two different lives, and I wasn't ready to be the standup guy she deserved. Even though she irked my fucking nerves and spent too much of my damn money, she had my heart. But at this point, she couldn't do anything to bring me my shit, so I had to stay on Lay's ass!

Man, I did everything in my power to get Lay's ass back on my team. From gifts, poems, to crying over the fucking phone, her ass was being stubborn. So, since she was being such an ass, I hollered at her so-called home girl Barney to see if she would be willing to help a nigga out. I always told Lay never trust that bitch, and sure enough, she jumped right on my dick. LITERALLY! I didn't have to finesse her like I did Lay, shit I barely

# Good Girlz With Hood Habits

had to pay the bitch; she just wanted attention and dick. No matter what I asked, she brought it in, plus the bitch had a mean ass head game. She did shit I never heard of, like one time the bitch sucked my dick upside down, while inside my cell. She swallowed and sucked my balls.

Her pussy was trash, though, to lose and not as wet as Lays or Rochelle's, but she was what I needed at the moment. As much as I hated to admit it, I missed Lay's spoiled ass. She was the one I could talk to about anything; she knew I wanted to own my own business and go back to school. Rochelle's ass didn't even care about my future; long as it didn't interfere with her shopping and not working, I could sell drugs to the day I die. Lay wanted more for me, more for us but, I couldn't leave the streets alone.

# Good Girlz With Hood Habits

Lay

I stopped talking to GM for three weeks, no calls, no text, no nothing even if I worked his building, I stayed far the fuck away from him. He sent messages, gifts, even had his uncle call me, but I was through; I felt like if you would ask me to do something like that and risk my freedom, then you didn't really fuck with me the way you said you did nor did you give a damn about my son. I'm not going to lie though; I missed his ass like crazy. But I heard he was fucking my so-called homegirl, you know the one that first told me about the numbers, yeah that bitch, he was fucking her.

# Good Girlz With Hood Habits

## GM

Besides all the other bull shit I had going on with Lay, my kids, and this jail shit, when I called my mom, she hit me with some fucked up news. My mother hit me with a heartbreaker, my grandmother, my lifeline, my heart died. I walked around with a cloud over my head for two days. I needed my best friend. I needed my Lay! I did what no locked up nigga fucking with a CO should ever do... I called my bitch on the bluebird, but Lay wasn't answering, and I needed her bad.

"You have a collect call from Bryan Rollins. To accept this call, press 0, to block future calls; press five."

"What GM!"

"Listen, bae, I can't talk much or about the situation, but I miss you. I know I was wrong, and I'm sorry, but I need you bae."

"GM, get off my phone. I know what this is, you need me to be your fool, and that's not me. I played the fool for far too long, and I'm...."

"LAY, just listen! Damn! My grandmother just died. I don't need you to do shit for me but listen. I'm going crazy in here, man, you not fucking with me, and I feel like I'm by myself. Fuck that

other shit. I only need you; I need my big head!"

I told myself that I was saying this shit to get her back

on my team, but in all honesty, it was the truth, I really did need

her. I got her to meet me in the ODR the next day, and with one

hug and a few promises, I had my girl back! Life was fucking

good again.

# Good Girlz With Hood Habits

Lay

On a Thursday, GM called my phone collect to tell me his grandmother died. I know we shouldn't have used the bluebird, but he said that was the only way to contact me because he had to flush his phone. Plus, I wasn't answering anyway. I felt bad for him because my uncle that helped raise me, and my brothers were battling cancer and didn't expect to live much longer. I agreed to meet him in the ODR the next day to talk.

GM got a job as the hall man so he could move freely through the jail in his green uniform. We couldn't talk as freely as we wanted, but I did get my point across, which was "I'm here for you but don't play me," he apologized, and I agreed to get a burner phone and set up the G4L collect service so we could talk. That night he sent his homeboy over to my house to get the rest of the shit I had and give me the money for the rent. I can't lie, his little friend was cute, and he tried to make conversation, but I shut that down real fast. I was a one-man woman, and my heart and pussy belonged to GM.

# Good Girlz With Hood Habits

## GM

The day came where I had to go to court to see what type of time I was going have to do for violating my probation. That's when shit hit the fan. Lay, Barney, and Rochelle came to court. Lay sat all the way in the back with glasses and a hat on. She really couldn't be seen because of her job. But Barney ass was front and center with a swollen fucking stomach! Yeah, that bitch was pregnant, but I wasn't claiming it until she got a DNA test, hell she was fucking the whole Southside of the jail. Fuck I look like claiming that baby. Rochelle's ass came in there with a "Free my husband "shirt on, with all four kids in toe. I saw Lay looking back and forth at Barney, Rochelle, and me. I saw tears coming down her face. I fucked up.

*Later that night.......*

"So, you're married, fucking with Barney, and got a whole fucking basketball team of kids?"

# Good Girlz With Hood Habits

"Lay, I can't even explain it, but shit with us wasn't supposed to even get to this point but yeah, what you said is true."

"Bryan, you a clown ass nigga for real, after all the shit I told you about, the bull shit I went through with my child's father, you turn around and do this shit to me? You lucky I don't get anybody to fuck your bitch ass up. I hope they throw the fucking book at your stupid ass. I'm so glad I stopped fucking you. Do you know Barney got more bodies under her belt than the Baltimore City Morgue? You are a wasted piece of fucking sperm. I hope you die bitch!"

"Damn Lay, that's how you feel? Never mind all the shit I've done for you. You're just going bark at me like that?"

"I'm so sick of you and your shit, yo!"

"So, what your spoiled ass going leave me now that a nigga got some fucking time? Huh, Lay, you going to leave me. Well, fuck you! Don't be with me after all I've done for your ass!"

With that, I hung up; I just needed her to be fucked up in the head so she would think I was really all about her. Shit, I got eight months to do, and out PA, there aren't any green dots or shots of 1 (weed) or 2 (tobacco). All the money I would get

would be from my mom and Lay, so I needed her ass; then,

after these eight months, I was cutting her loose.

***Over the next eight months………***

When I tell you, my life was fucking crazy since I was

sent to PA that wouldn't even halfway explain the shit going on.

First, I found out Lay started fucking with another nigga. She left

my ass alone four months into my bid. What we didn't know

was she was pregnant with a little girl. She was due the day I

came home. I didn't know how I felt about the baby to tell you

the truth. See, I still loved Lay and would have loved to keep her

around, but I just couldn't.  Anyway, I heard Lay was doing her

thing on the up and up tip and was on her way to becoming a

Captain at the jail, I think. I was happy for her but missed her

like shit. Besides my woman troubles, I heard through the jail

walls that some little nigga name Lamar took over my hood,

moving weight and cutting all my street soldiers' throat with his

dirt-cheap prices and a good grade of coke. If I didn't know any

better, I would have thought Lay might have put some nigga on

# Good Girlz With Hood Habits

while I was down, but I know the bitch ain't that hood or dumb

to fuck with my shit; she knew better then to cross me, or did

she?

# Good Girlz With Hood Habits

Lay

Once GM caught his time, I left all that jail shit alone. I was up for another promotion but decided to take a step back from Corrections. I took a leave of absence from the jail and decided to move to California. Amid all this shit, I forgot to tell y'all about my trust fund. When I met up with my dad's lawyer, I was informed that my dad left me $1.5 million. No one knew he had that much money, not even my mom. I was his only daughter, so he left me everything, including a 4-bedroom house in DC. I got the check a couple of months after I started messing with GM. I never told him about the money, honestly, I forgot about it. I was too busy chasing after GM and making sure he was good. So, to say I was living good without the jail or GM was an understatement.

When I left Baltimore, Harlem was turning six. His father had been trying to get in contact with me, and I finally let him facetime him from time to time. He supposedly was going to anger management classes and had a job at Downtown Locker Room in Towson. He asked could we get back together, and every time I told him the same thing, NO! GM spoiled my ass, and I wasn't going back to no regular-ass nigga. Plus, I was in California, fuck was I going do with a nigga living in Baltimore making minimum wage. What GM didn't know, though, was I had been hitting his stash every time he had me make a drop-off; I would pay myself $500, and that was at least three times a week plus he thought my rent was $2200 instead of $1500.

Every month for seven months, I was bringing in an extra $6700 besides my regular salary. The last time I checked my wall safe, I had a little over forty stacks, a quarter of coke, and a pound of loud. Along with 1.5 million dollars in my bank account. This the type of shit you read about in Urban Novels; shit like this doesn't usually happen to me. Another thing I didn't tell GM was I was using his connect to help my little brother start his empire on the streets. I started fucking Bobbie to get lower prices for my brother. No one knew it was me that funded my brother's operation; well, it was GM's money that funded it, but you get what I'm saying. The crazy and probably fucked up thing about me putting my brother on was he took over GM's old blocks. Yeah, I loved GM, but he showed me a

new life, and I wanted the money, fuck love. Love got me a

bastard baby and bad credit. No fuck love, plus GM thought his

ass was slick. I knew him, and Barney was fucking around, and

this bitch was going up to PA to visit his ass too. I wanted to

forward all those Corrlinks emails to her ass so bad, but I said

fuck it, I was on a money-making mission.

My brother Lamar was doing his thing on the streets of

Baltimore while I was living it up in Cali. My account was

growing. My life was far more exciting than I ever thought it

would be. I was buying any and everything I wanted. I switched

my cars up again and moved out of my condo. When I came

back to home, I would be living in the house my dad left me. I

felt like Ace from Paid in Full on some Money-making Mitch shit

"Life was Good." But no matter how low key you were or how

nice you tried to be, there's always going to be a glitch thrown

in the program. I wished I would have thought about that

before I ever agreed to be GM's girl. One day I was coming

home and found an envelope on my doorstep that contained

pictures of me and GM fucking in the day room of G section and my discharged papers from when I lost me and GM's baby. Last but not least was a 3D sonogram picture of the little girl I was carrying now looking just like her daddy. Oh, did I forget to mention Harlem was going be a big brother?

**Kei' To Da Bankz**

# Good Girlz With Hood Habits

## Kei'sha

At 25 years old, I would like to think I made pretty good choices for myself. I'm single, financially independent, and a boss. Hey world, I'm Kei'sha (pronounced Keisha) Williams. Lay is my baby cousin, I know her story was pretty crazy, and you only read half so far. We lost contact when I went away to school, but trust I'm getting baby cousin back to the queen she truly is. Anyway, for now, let me introduce you to my world. As I said, I'm pretty freaking dope. Maybe a little lonely, but other than that, my world is fucking great. It wasn't always like that; I've had my ups and downs over the years, but fuck it, I made it.

I'm currently in my last year in law school. I work at an upcoming law office here in Baltimore. It's an all-female law office run by professional strong black women. I've been here for two years as a clerk; however, after graduation, there's a job here waiting for me as an attorney. So, you see, I didn't have time for distractions. My social life was dead. I was in school full time and worked full time. I've been like this since I was young. My work ethic was out of this world. And honestly, I didn't have to work. My father was a King Pen, and my family was very comfortable financially; however, I always got it on my own.

My mom was one of the first female detectives in Baltimore County back in the late '70s. She met my dad in 1984 while on vacation in Miami; they dated off and on for two years before my dad convinced my mom to move to Miami with him. My mom had my oldest brother Paul by her high school sweetheart when she was off with my dad (some family members swear Paul is really my dad's son). My brother's father was killed when Paul was nine months; a number run gone wrong. My dad adopted Paul in 85, then I was born and 88, followed by my twin sisters in 89. Although my mom became a stay at home wife and mother, she never stopped teaching her kids about hustling and grinding. She especially taught my sisters and me never to depend on a man; she always had a stash on the side that only I knew about for rainy days.

My dad was a bonafide drug dealer, and he didn't care who knew about it. He had cops on payroll, and a Columbian connect. (This connect will come in handy later on for Lay. Stay

# Good Girlz With Hood Habits

tuned.) We lived like royalty in Miami, my dad's oldest brother Edward Calvin Williams was point guard for the Miami Heat from 1988 to 1993 when he retired from the league and moved to New York with his wife and oldest daughter Tiffany. My dad got caught up in some IRS tax evasion shit, so he sent me, my mother, and two sisters to New York to live with my uncle in 1999.

I hated New York; the streets were dirty, people were loud and mean, and we had to move in with my uncle and his family. Mind you, my uncle's house was a nice 3-bedroom condo with two bathrooms and a den. But we were used to a house, our own bed, and bathrooms, so when we came here and had to share, I wasn't with it at all. My uncle had three daughters, Tiffany, by his first wife YoYo and Lauren (aka Renz) and London (aka Lolo) by his second wife, Caryll. We never really dealt with Tiffany's mom; she was drama and left my uncle to be a single dad. Tiffany's mom was a known escort in Miami, but Unc fell for the high yellow bombshell; she was able to snatch him up, get married, and have a baby all within two years. When they moved to NYC, Yoyo fell in love with the fast

life, divorced my uncle, and left him to take care of Tiffany. Tiff

was seven when Unc remarried and ten when the twins came.

We moved in the same year the twins were born. Here we are

three adults, four kids, and two newborn babies in a three-

bedroom apartment in Manhattan, NY. When we left Miami, my

mom had 300k stashed of her own money. I begged her to buy

us our own place, but because she didn't have a job, we

couldn't jump out there without suspicions.

My dad ended up getting sentenced to ten years for tax

evasion, fraud, and embezzlement. My mom divorced him two

years into his bid, not because she didn't love him, but for

financial freedom, everything tied to him was seized, and we

were broke. Well, on paper, it appeared we were broke. After

graduating from middle school, we moved to Towson,

Maryland; by then, my mom got a job with the Baltimore

County Police Department working in the records department. I

was 15, Paul was 17, and my twin sisters were 14. Paul was back

with us because he stayed in Miami with my uncle while we

# Good Girlz With Hood Habits

were in New York. My mom was able to stack and save her money the three and a half years we lived with my Uncle, so her 300k grew, and we were able to buy our house straight cash. I went to Carver High School and took up cosmetology as a trade. It wasn't what I was passionate about, but they didn't have many other options, so I went with that.

In my tenth-grade year, I met my first boyfriend, Nico. He was my neighbor's cousin that came down to Maryland from New Jersey for the summer. He was my first love. He taught me how to make love; at 17, Nico played with my body as if he was a grown-ass man, and I would give my last breath to feel his dick in my stomach. Nico was a year older than me and lived a rough life. What attracted me to him was his smile; he could light up a room. At 16, I was still a virgin, but Nico ended that the first summer he came around. We never really were official; Nico was in love with the streets, and my momma would have killed me if she knew I was dealing with him because he had ties to gang members. But every summer until my senior year, Nico spent nights in my bed when my mother would fall asleep. Nico

# Good Girlz With Hood Habits

was the first one who taught me how to hustle besides my momma.

Nico had me working part-time in a hair salon in Baltimore after school and on Saturdays. What I didn't know was that the shop I was working in was his child's mother. Hell, I didn't even know he had a kid until he died years later. Nico helped me get my first car, a red 87 Saab with gold VVS wheels and a soft drop-top. My mom thought a kid's father from my school sold it to me. How the hell else was I going to explain that type of car? Hell, she didn't even know I had 27k saved by the time I was in the 12th grade. My last year in high school was bittersweet; the second week of my senior year, Nico was shot on Woodridge and Greenmount. He left me alone. He was the only guy I had been with, my first love. Yet it was so much that I didn't know about him, like he was five years older than me, had two kids, and a wife. I was just his summer plaything. I owe that man so much though; he taught me so much in so little time.

# Good Girlz With Hood Habits

Nothing Nico owned belonged to me. No one but his best friend Pookie, and sister knew who I was and what I meant to him. His youngest sister India knew how much her brother loved me. At his funeral, she gave me an envelope with the title to my car, an insurance policy with me as his beneficiary, and a key to the house next door to my mom. Come to find out the house belonged to Nico the whole time. He left me the house, two cars, and an insurance policy worth $75k; I was set and was barely 18. I didn't know how I would keep this from my mother, she didn't know I was fucking that grown-ass man, and she surely wouldn't understand how I was sitting on a small fortune at such a young age. My cousin Tiffany was a year older than me and was attending Morgan State University, which wasn't far from my house. She knew about Nico and helped me many times sneak him in my house or hide the hickeys he put on me. So, I went to her for help.

"Tiff, what I'm going to do with a fucking house and two more cars?"

"Kei, I can't believe that man left you all that shit; your little

pussy must be powerful."

"Yo, be for real, please. And have you ever cashed an insurance

policy in? How the fuck do I do that?"

"Just sell all that shit, matter fact, give me one of those cars so I

can stop driving that raggedy Ford Taurus."

"You can have my car, but you are not getting none of Nico

cars." Nico left me with a 2005 Lexus GS and a 2006 Audi S4; I

wasn't giving them up.

"Well, how the hell are you going explain two brand new luxury

cars to your mother? You know what, call Uncle Cruddy, you

know he'll help you."

"Oh, damn, I forgot about Uncle Cruddy, he'll come through for

real."

My Uncle Cruddy was my mom's brother, he lived in

Atlanta but traveled all over the world. He was a top-selling real

estate agent and worked with the best of the best. When I

called him, he was on his way to Maryland to look at a few

properties near Baltimore City's Inner Harbor, so he agreed to

# Good Girlz With Hood Habits

meet with me. Uncle Cruddy was the oldest brother of five

boys; my mother was the only girl. Her mother and father

adopted her when she was 13 weeks old from a 15-year-old

church member that was molested by her stepfather. Even

though she was adopted, no one treated her any differently.

Uncle Cruddy met me at my school during third period; I didn't

want my mom to know I was meeting with him.

"Look at my baby girl, how have you been, Rudy?" (Rudy was a

family nickname of mine.)

"I've been good, Unc, I need your help with something, and I

can't talk to momma or daddy about it."

"Oh shit, you are not pregnant, are you? I thought I taught you

about protection and staying away from these knuckleheads."

"No, Unc, I'm not pregnant. Do you remember Nico that would

come up here during the summer?'

"Yeah, lil brown skin dude next door, that got killed, what about

him?"

"Well, we were dating during the summers, and when he died, he left me with a house, two cars, and an insurance policy worth 75k."

"Get the fuck out of here, Rudy, you had to be given that young man something other than time. Everything is in your name?"

"Yeah, and I don't know what to do with it. That's why I called you. Can you sell that house for me? I want to keep the car, but I don't know how I can explain it to momma."

"This is what we are going to do, I'll sell the house as a quick sale, you won't get as much, but it'll be fast. You said you got two cars, right? Take one back upstate, store it in my garage, the one you keep we'll just tell your mom it was a graduation gift from me. What are you going to do about the car you have now?"

"I'm giving it to Tiff. What about the insurance policy?"

"Cash it out and put it up. Rudy, you're about to have a lot of money at your disposal for a girl your age, be smart about it."

# Good Girlz With Hood Habits

My uncle was right. By the time I graduated high school, I had a bank account with $253k in it that no one knew about. I still worked at the hair salon on the weekends, Nico's wife moved to Florida after his death, her sister ran the salon, and neither one knew about my relationship with Nico or the money I had. I worked there up until I left for college. I got a full ride to the University of Maryland College Park and was going to be living on campus. My mother and father gave me my college fund as a graduation gift since they didn't have to pay for college. My dad was now at the Federal Halfway house, so he was back in my life. When I checked in my dorm on August 03, 2007, I had a 2005 Audi S4, my tuition, room and board, and books all paid for, and a sitting on $397k.

To say I was straight was an understatement. My college experience wasn't anything special. I didn't date or go to the parties on campus. I did my work and stayed to myself. The one time I did give a nigga a chance, he was a fucking nut-ball. Like real shit, the dude had mental problems and became obsessed with me. He was what my grandmother would call a wolf in sheep's clothing. I missed all the red flags.

I worked at the school's diner; I didn't need the money. I worked there so I wouldn't get bored. I was on the Dean's List and was set to graduate a year early because I went to school all year round. Anyway, I was working my usual Friday night at the diner when this group of well-dressed men came in and was seated in my section. They all looked like young professionals, with tailored suits on, and few had briefcases. They ordered their food, and my eyes met the eyes of this chocolate god! He was 6'4, 220lbs of solid muscle dark chocolate with dimples, he wore his hair close cut and his suit fit him to a tee. He was fine! Ever since Nico passed, I didn't date and I never really looked at guys, but this man sitting in my face was the alpha and omega; he lit a fire in me that had been out for almost three years now.

Eric was his name; he said he was a teacher's assistant on campus, but I'd never seen him. This man was pure perfection, or so I thought. He introduced himself to me once his party was about to leave the restaurant and asked could he take me out. I said no, I wasn't ready to date, and I was in gear to graduate at the end of this school year; I didn't need any distractions in my life. But Eric was persistent. Every Friday, he came to the diner and ordered a root beer float and fries. He always tipped over the 18% required and left his number on the receipt. It took three months before I agreed to go on a date with him, but I did.

It was a cool crisp November evening when Eric took me to this little jazz restaurant that was the fucking worst to me. I'm 21 years old, why the fuck would you take me to listen to jazz? I wasn't feeling it at all. The date was horrible, and I knew there wouldn't be another one. After getting in my car and driving off, I deleted his number and forgot all about him. Three weeks later, I walked into the diner, and it was filled with yellow and white roses.

"Wow, where did these come from?" I asked my coworker, and she looked at me like I had two damn heads. I didn't know what the fuck this bitch problem was, but she could keep that attitude to her damn self.

# Good Girlz With Hood Habits

"They're for you, from a guy named Eric."

"You read my card?"

She rolled her eyes and walked away. Fucking hater. Eric apologized for the date and went on and on about how he was nervous about dating me and wanted another chance. Something in my stomach told me to say no, but I didn't listen. I accepted his apology and went out with him again. Lord, was that a big fucking mistake. Eric had serious insecurities; he called me at least ten times a day and texted triple that. After three months of his ass, I blocked him and changed my number. I thought that was the end of it, but this nigga showed up at my job, my classes, and followed me every day. Mind you; I never gave his ass any pussy. Could you imagine how he would act had he got some of this pussy? I had to eventually let the job at the diner go because he kept popping up. I even traded my car in and changed my number at least two more times. He got the hint, or at least I thought he did, when I put a restraining order out on his ass.

# Good Girlz With Hood Habits

I went six months without hearing from him then I started getting collect calls from a mental institution. This fool was locked up in the psych ward. Where the fuck did this nigga come from? I blocked the institution from calling me and again got a new number. I started working at the law firm not too long after that. On my first day on the job, we had to see a client at Baltimore City Detention Center, and that's when I met the finest man I've ever seen in my life. Bishop King was tall, dark, and handsome. He had a swagger to him that I couldn't explain. He walked like he ruled the world. And little did I know this nigga really did.

The first day I met him, he never said two words to me; even when I talked to him, he just nodded and kept it moving. My boss did most of the talking during that first visit. That night I went home and fucked myself silly thinking of Bishop. He had been sitting in this pretrial facility for four years. When I looked over his case, I didn't understand why he was even sitting in jail. The state failed to find enough evidence and the case kept getting postponed. Surely any lawyer could have gotten him out or at least a slap on the wrist. Something about the whole case

felt wrong, and like we were getting into some shit, we had no

business getting involved in.

# Good Girlz With Hood Habits

## Bishop

"You motherfuckers getting really relaxed with my fucking money."

"B, it's not us, them niggas on the southside fucking shit up."

"How the fuck you sound, you letting another nigga stop your money? All this shit is illegal, fuck you mean they fucking shit up. Y'all niggas doing the most but ain't doing shit. Get the fuck out my cell."

Sorry about that, let me introduce myself, I'm Bishop King, but y'all can call me Bankz. As you read already, I currently reside at the Baltimore City Detention Center. I know what you're thinking, and yes, I'm everything you fucking think. I'm a young, getting money motherfucker. Even behind these dirty ass walls, I get to the bag. You see, I run the Northside of this jail, from drugs to pussy, I sell it inside this jail and uptown. I've been sitting in this jail for four years, building my empire. Inside these walls, I can sell a dime bag of weed that's $10 uptown for $50 in here. I take a buk strip, split it in half, and make $200 alone, and niggas get buks uptown for less than $20. So yeah,

I'm getting money motherfucker.

I know I shouldn't be here hell, I went to law school. I

could have defended myself, but I needed to get on the inside

to make power moves. You see, on the streets I was mid-level,

don't get me wrong I was getting money, and my name was

ringing bells, but my shit wasn't banging like I wanted them to

be. I was a greedy motherfucker. But here in this jail, I am a god.

I have CO's on my payroll and the entire administration staff in

my back pocket. I made about $30,000 a week after paying off

everyone. Another reason I was so stuck on being in this hell

hole was because I had no family uptown.

My mom died giving birth to me, and my pops were

doing football numbers with the Feds. I'm an only child, and the

rest of my family never acknowledged me. My dad is white and

seven years older than my mom, so when my 17-year-old

mother came home with this white nigga, my mom's people

weren't having it, so they kicked her out. When she died, no

one came to my rescue. It was my dad and me until I was 15,

then he got knocked, and I've been on my own ever since. I don't have kids, honestly; I don't want any. I just want to get money. I will say this, that damn Kei'sha has been on my mind since she left this morning. A nigga like me needs her on his team. She's sexy, smart as fuck, and look like she'll hold a nigga down. I could see myself marrying her ass. Shit, I never even thought about marriage. Can I tell y'all a secret? Y'all asses better not laugh either! I'm a virgin.

# Good Girlz With Hood Habits

## Kei'sha

Bishop stayed on my mind more than I care to admit. I knew nothing would ever come from that, so I chose to push Bishop and his fine ass to the back of my mind. I had graduation coming up, and I wanted to focus on finishing this last milestone of mine.

"Girl, you never go out, come on and hit the strip with me."

"Tiff if you don't get your high yellow ass off my bed with your street clothes on, I'm going to knock your ass on the floor."

"Kei, ain't nobody scared of you, now come on, please."

"No, Tiff, I'm tired, and I have to go to work in the morning."

"You don't have to stay long; come on, let's celebrate. You graduate soon, and I just got a new job. Please lil cuz."

"Ard damn, but I'm only there for two hours max!"

"Bet say no more, get dressed and not in no damn suit either Kei!"

"I know how to dress for the club, Tiff damn, now get off my bed!"

# Good Girlz With Hood Habits

I walked to my closet to see what I could throw on; I had a closet full of work attire but no real "street" clothes. I settled on a pair of destroyed ash wash bell-bottom jeans, a simple white cami, and a pair of Tory Burch sandals. My hair reached the middle of my back, so I decided to let it hang out. I don't wear makeup, so I did a little gloss and put my big hoops in and was ready to go.

"You look real cute cousin."

"Thanks, Tiff, shit next to you, I look like a schoolteacher."

My cousin had on a strapless all-black dress that came just under the cuff of her ass with some 6-inch heels that tied up her leg and a long ass weave. Now I know I look good, but Tiff was definitely giving me a run for my money. We decided to catch a cab instead of driving so that we both can have a drink or two. Getting to the club, we didn't have to wait in line because Tiff knew the bouncer. I must admit it; it was nice to let my hair down and enjoy myself. I was dancing with some random guy when the bartender walked over to me and handed me a phone. I was confused as fuck because Tiff was right next to me, and no one else knew where I was.

"Sorry, you must have the wrong person I shouted over the music."

"Nah, ma this for you, and I think you should get on the phone before we all end up dead."

Now I was fucking confused.

"Hello!'

"Are you having a good time, Ms. Kei'sha?"

"OMG! It was Bishop," I thought to myself.

"How did you know I was here, wait, how are you calling me? What the fuck?"

"Never mind all that, baby girl, listen tell homeboy behind you to back up before he loses his life." I started looking around, trying to see if I saw him.

"No need to look for me, baby girl, I'm still in this hell hole, just know I got eyes everywhere, so again tell homey to back up, or it's lights out."

Soon as I turned around, I saw two red dots on the guy's shirt.

# Good Girlz With Hood Habits

"Bishop, what the fuck? Sir, can you please leave? I don't want to see you get hurt," I said to the man while still holding the phone to my ear. Luckily, he walked away.

"Now, baby girl, we haven't had much time together but believe me when I say you got a man, and it's me. Next time you take your ass out to a club with that little ass shirt on, and those fucking jeans on, I'm going to blow that bitch up. Grab your homegirl and get the fuck out now before I get upset."

"Bishop, I think you have lost your damn mind. I'm going to forget this ever happened, and I'm going to continue my fucking night." With that said, I gave the phone back and walked away to finish having a good time.

Thirty minutes after that little incident, the music stopped playing, and the DJ announced the club would be closing due to a small kitchen fire. Something told me this was Bishop's doing. As we were waiting for our cab to come, this big ass black truck pulled up.

"Yo, Kei'sha, Bish said to get in."

"Who the fuck is that? And who the fuck is Bish?" Tiff asked.

"Hell, if I know, come on, the cab is pulling up."

I jumped in the cab so fucking fast; I couldn't believe the one fucking night I decide to go out, I have to deal with a nigga that's not even my fucking nigga, and to top it off, this nigga is in jail! Now I've heard of some crazy shit before, but this was ridiculous. I walked to my house, and there the same big ass man from the club was sitting on my porch.

"Kei'sha Bishop is on the phone."

"You can tell Bishop to leave me alone and stay away from me, like what the fuck? I don't even know that man."

"Kei'sha, if you don't shut all that shit up and talk to your fucking man, I promise you I'll break out this fucking jail and come fuck you up," Bishop hollered through the speaker.

"What Bishop? You acting really crazy; first off, how did you even know where I was, and why are you doing this? I barely know you, and if you haven't noticed, I'm out here in the free world, and your ass is locked up. How are you supposed to be my man?"

# Good Girlz With Hood Habits

"Kei, you and I both know my reach is long, and this jail shit is a small obstacle to a giant. I'm feeling you, lil momma, and I want you now. We can do this the easy way, or the hard way, know every nigga you fuck with is going to die, so can you live with niggas blood on your hands?"

"Bishop, this is crazy, you could have just sent flowers or something nigga, you ain't have to do all this, shit."

"Girl, you funny as shit. Listen, I gotta go, but you heard what I said. I fucks with you Kei'sha, and I'm always going overboard for mine. Yo, Sin, you can go my nigga good looking out."

"No doubt that's lil sis now, I got you."

With that, he walked away and went to his truck.

"Oh, Kei' Bishop wanted me to give you this."

This man walked back to me with a duffle bag. I didn't even bother looking in it. I walked in my house with Tiff staring me in my damn face.

"So, bitch when you start messing with niggas in jail?"

"Oh, shut up, Tiff, you heard the whole conversation. I don't mess with that man. And honestly, he got me scared as fuck."

"Girl, he fucks with you heavy, he ready to start killing mother fuckers for you. This sounds like some shit we read in a book or something. Wait, what's in the bag? What the nigga moving in?"

"Hell no, Tiff, he's in jail!"

"Just open the damn bag, smartass."

I picked the bag up and placed it on the counter near my kitchen. Well, I will be damn; it was a bag full of money with a note.

Kei,

It's $100k in this bag; it's yours. Keep it 100 with me, and there's 100 more for you.

~Bankz


"Ask his ass if he has a friend. I can't believe it, Kei; I don't know what you do to these men, but you need to teach a class or something. First, Nico, now this Bishop/Bankz guy."

I honestly was speechless. Where did he get this kind of money from? Why give it to me? I know he said he was feeling me, but damn I can't imagine what he'd give if he loved my ass.

# Good Girlz With Hood Habits

This was crazy. This doesn't happen to regular people. Bishop was putting in me a real bad headspace, and I needed to clear my head. Clearly, we came from two different worlds, and I wasn't sure if mixing the two would be a good idea.

"So, what are you going to do Kei?"

"I don't know, Tiff, I'm a part of his legal team; there's definitely a conflict of interest there, plus he's in jail. I know we are going to get him out, but can I be a 'trappers' girlfriend? Nico was different because I had no idea what was going on. I need to go to sleep and forget this night even happened."

"Maybe you should talk to Auntie, I mean her being married to your dad for so many years, I know she picked up some street smarts she can give you."

"Yeah, you right, I need my mom to make sense of this for me because this is a bit much for me. Go with me in the morning; I think it's time I tell her everything anyway."


*The next day.......*

"Hey, girls, what are y'all doing here?"

Page 119

# Good Girlz With Hood Habits

"Hey, Auntie, did you cook?"

"Tiff, I swear you would think you are 300 lbs. the way you eat, lol it's some leftovers in the fridge." Tiff ran to the kitchen.

"Hey momma, you got a minute to talk? I need your opinion and need to tell you something."

"Baby, you know I always have time for my baby girl, what's going on?"

"Ma, do you remember Nico from next door?"

"Girl, I know you are not about to tell me about that girl and money he left you."

"Mommy, you knew about it?"

"Who do you think set it up? How else would he get your information even to list you on an insurance policy? KeiWei (her nickname for me) Nico told me about you two the first time he stayed the night. I hope you didn't think you were that slick."

"Maaaaa, I can't believe you knew all this time. I was scared to tell you. Why didn't you say anything?"

"I figured you'd tell me when you were ready. Now, what else do you need to talk about?"

# Good Girlz With Hood Habits

I told my mom all about Bishop, the night at the club, the money, and my feelings for him.

"I can tell you this KeiWei; he's not going to stop. From what you told me, he's solid like Nico was, and he wants you, and it seems like you want him too. I get it's a conflict of interest, and I don't want you to jeopardize your career in no way. I will say this, you better get him out, and soon because the way you smile when you say his name, it's only so long before you fall for him, and a jailhouse relationship is not what you want."

My mom was right, I wanted Bishop's ass, not because of his money, but I saw something in his eyes; his walk spoke to me, and I could see me drowning in his arms. I needed that man, and I would be damn if I didn't get him.

# Good Girlz With Hood Habits

Bishop

It's been one month since I met Kei'sha. One month since I decided she was mine. In that one month, I had to send my shooters her way twice, once at some club and the other to her office. Kei'sha thought I was playing when I said she was mine. She started ducking a nigga after what happened at the club. So, I had Sin swing pass her job and let her know at the next meeting with my lawyer her ass better be there, or I was breaking out of this mother fucker to come to get her. After that second visit, she got it together and was sitting in front of me now looking so fucking good in a black pencil skirt and white blouse. Nothing too extra, simple, and classic is how I'd describe her look.

"So, Bishop, we were able to get all the evidence, witness, and documentation we need, and I'm confident that at your next court date, you'll be a free man."

"Good looking out Heather, when do we go to court?"

"The soonest we could get you in front of the judge was September 19th."

# Good Girlz With Hood Habits

"Are you kidding me? That's three months from now, what the fuck I'm going to do in this hell hole for three months?"

"I know it's not ideal, but that's the best I could do; they wanted to push it back to after the new year."

"Man, I guess it's better than nothing, shit I guess I'll just put my big toe in the air and chill out. Thanks again, Heather, and you to Ms. Williams." I winked at her, oblivious to my attorney, she rolled her eyes and walked out.

"Hey, Ms. Williams, you think I could get your card or something, some of these niggas in here might need your services."

"Ummm, I don't have any, besides I'm not a lawyer yet, just an aid."

"That's what up; ladies have a good day."

I walked out of the room, smiling. I already had all of Kei'sha's information; hell, I knew the day she had to take the bar exam. You see, I have never wanted a woman this bad in my life, and when I say never, I mean NEVER FUCKING EVER. Kei'sha felt like home, that's the only way I can describe it. I felt peace when I talked to her or was around her. My whole mood

changed. I guess you are wondering how I got through this

world making all this money and still be a virgin. It's simple since

I was a kid; my goal was money. I got head all the time, but I

never slipped in any pussy. The one time I tried, the girl pussy

smelled like crab legs and earring backs, and it turned me off.

So, until I met Kei'sha, I never really thought about pussy like

that, besides, I've been in this hell hole for damn near four

years, I wasn't fucking nothing in here. CO's always threw pussy

at me, but these bitches was nasty and fucked in these dirty ass

cells with these dirty ass niggas, I'll pass. As I'm walking down

thru the 40, I saw a few niggas I was cool with from J-section.

"My nigga Bankz, what's good?"

"Yo, I heard your niggas fucking up my money."

"Now you know we move the same; I stay on my side, you stay

on yours. Niggas eating good on my side ya dig?"

"I ain't tripping matter fact I need to holla at you on some shit.

But not right now. Hit the jimmy mack after the count. Shit bout

to change, and I need you on top of shit ya dig?"

# Good Girlz With Hood Habits

"Say no more."

Kutez was my nigga from uptown; we use to go to Northern together, dude was solid and loyal. I was going to give him control over my part of the jail. He was facing football numbers, so he would be good, plus niggas respected him. Walking back on my tier, I noticed we had a new CO on the post, niggas was about to trash on his dumb ass. I get to my cell, and there was a note on my bunk, which was fucking odd. Nobody would even dare come in my cell, so I head to the next cell over.

"One of yall niggas leave this on my bunk?"

"Nah, Bankz, niggas ain't been in your cell."

I brushed the shit off like it wasn't anything. Niggas knew not to fuck with me. I went and got my hygiene shit and headed to the shower. As much as I was happy to get out and hit the ground running, I was a little nervous. I've been here for four years, I made money here, and as fucked up as it sounded, these niggas were the only family I had. Then there was Kei'sha, I knew for sure I wanted her, and this jail shit was the only thing holding her from me. But was I ready to be with a woman for

real? Like what do I do when she gets on my nerves? This

shower had me feeling all types of shit. I dried off, put my

shower shoes on, and went back to my cell. Once I put my

sweats and a t-shirt on, I laid back and opened the note that

was left on my bed.

*Bishop,*

*You're not the only one that can find someone.*

*Listen, I'm not used to your world, but I like you.*

*Teach me your world.*

*But don't hurt me.*

*~Kei*

This woman was full of surprises, I see. But if it was my

world, she wanted it was my world she was going to get.

# Good Girlz With Hood Habits

Kei'sha

I know y'all thinking I'm crazy, hell I think I may have lost my mind too, but something about Bishop had me doing the unthinkable. I had my cousin Lay find out where he slept and put the note on his bunk. Lay told me a little about him and his status in the jail. She also told me about the shit she was going through with her dude, and I thought she was fucking crazy. Ain't no way in hell was I breaking the law to be with Bishop, but from what Lay was telling me, I wouldn't have to because Bishop was stamped. Whatever the fuck that was supposed to mean.

Bishop had three months before he got out, and, at that time, I wanted to know as much as I could about him. So, we played 21 questions literally. Every morning I'd text his phone from a burner I brought just for him. And by the time I got off, he would text me back his replies. At night he would text me his 21 questions, and, in the morning, I would have his reply. We did that for the first month. By the time the second month, came around we knew damn near everything about each other.

# Good Girlz With Hood Habits

Bishop decided if we were going to be together, I needed to know all about his business, so he put me in "boot camp."

Every evening when I got off, Sin would pick me up and take me to the gun range, sometimes Lay and Tiff would go with me. Sin taught me how to load, unload, and shoot for two hours a day. Bishop had me reading books on business like his drug empire was a real fortune 500 company. I met all his workers from uptown and saw where his trap houses were. Sin introduced me to a few of the heavy hitters that were down with Bishop's crew. I saw so much work that needed to be done. Like for starters, Bishop was paying two different sets of people to do the same job, his trap houses were like party houses that just happened to sell drugs, and his connect was overcharging him for stepped on work. You see, Bishop didn't know who my father was, nor did he know I knew the game; I just chose not to broadcast it. I still kept in contact with a few people Nico introduced me to, so I went and hollered at his old connect.

"I can't believe it, is it little Kei' standing before me?"

"Hey Dam, what have you been up too?"

# Good Girlz With Hood Habits

"I'm good, baby girl, damn you grew up, fuck you doing down here on the mount? You straight, you need something?"

"Dam, I need you to keep it 100 with me, I'm about to ask you some shit, and you, one of the only people I know, won't sugar coat shit."

"You damn right, what's up, baby girl?"

"Do you know a dude named Bankz?"

"Hell yeah, everybody knows that nigga, why what's up?"

"That's my nigga; we have been dealing with each other for about two months. He's coming home in a few, and I want to know if he's the truth."

"Baby girl, that nigga tech, if that's your nigga you forever straight."

"Bet, my next question. If I was to get him to switch his connect, can you get me 15 kilo's a month for less than 18 per key?"

"What the fuck? I know Bankz don't know you out here on some Queen Pin shit? Baby girl, what are you doing?"

# Good Girlz With Hood Habits

"It's for Bankz, his connect is over charging, and I remember Nico saying if it's stepped on more than once the shit trash and Dam that shit some trash."

"Baby girl, you sure about this?"

"Yeah, I'm sure. Could you do it?"

"Yeah, it's nothing, tell that nigga get at me when he gets out. I can get him 15 a month for 16 a piece."

"Dam, walk me to my car."

When we got to my trunk, I popped it and gave him a duffle bag.

"Dam, it's $250k in there, I want the purest you have and bring them to the house Nico left for me."

"Kei' are you serious right now?"

"Yeah, when have you known me not to be serious?"

"Kei, why are you riding around Baltimore with this type of money? Meet me in an hour at Nico's old spot. Are you out here naked?"

"No, I got my 22 in my purse."

# Good Girlz With Hood Habits

"Kei, what the hell are you going do with a 22? Here take this Glock; if shit doesn't even feel right, you blast this mother fucker. Take Barclay all the way up till you get to the Library, hop on York Rd, and I'll be behind in less than an hour. Kei, if anything feel out of place, peel off and call me ard!"

"Yeah, Dam, I got it."

"Kei, be careful; Nico will reach out the grave and kill me if shit happens to you. Keep your head on a swivel."

I hopped in my car and did what Dam told me to. Dam knew my brother and always had our backs. I knew I could trust him with what I was doing. Just to explain to y'all what I was doing, I was upgrading my nigga. The money he gave me, I put with $150k of my own money and doubled up his reup. Bankz operation wasn't doing 15 a month; they barely were doing five in a month. But I was getting rid of theses niggas. I talked to Sin and my dad about what I was doing. My dad was against it at first, but he saw shit my way after I explained profit margins increasing and productivity creating more supply and demand. Sin had become another brother to me, and I introduced him to my real brother. Paul, Sin, and Bankz knew each other, so the partnership clicked right away.


*1 hour later......*

Sitting in front of Nico's old house brought back so many thoughts. I know he would be proud of me for going to law school, but would he agree to me being a fucking Queen Pin? I didn't plan on being in the game, I loved my career, and I had never broken the law before tonight, but it needed to be done. I promised myself that once Bankz's was out, I'd go back to my usual self. The shit sounded good. Dam pulled up behind my car in a Silver Dodge Grand Caravan with this dude named Kris. Kris was another friend of Nico's, we weren't close like Dam and me, but he didn't play about me either.

"Kei, open the trunk."

Dam took the money, and Kris came to the driver's side of my car.

"Kei, get out and take my car to your mom's place. Stay the night and go home in the morning."

# Good Girlz With Hood Habits

"What the fuck is going on?"

Now I was a little confused like I know niggas wasn't about to drag on me. Kris must have read my mind because he addressed my concerns.

"Girl, if you don't get your ass out of this car, we got 20 kilos in this damn van, you think we letting you put it in your car, a Benz at that, what are you trying to go to jail? News flash, lil sis, they are not going to house you and Bankz together."

"You so damn stupid. Don't scratch my shit, or you buying me another one."

"Lil sis, this is a 2010 Benz, I could buy you six of these with the cash in my pocket, don't insult me."

"Can y'all come the fuck on before we all be sitting in Central Bookings damn! Dam hollered out the window."

I left and went to my mom's house. She and my dad were in Miami for the next two weeks, so the place was empty. My last year in undergrad, my dad was released from the halfway house and moved my mom and sisters to a house in Timonium, Maryland. They remarried last year and have been traveling the world ever since. Making up for the lost time, I guess. I didn't have a room in this house; however, my twin sisters still lived here, so I went to their area in the house.

My dad had the house renovated, and the twins had the entire upstairs. They had the walls knocked down and made the top part of the house like a two-bedroom apartment for the twins. I laid on my sister Lon bed and thought about what I was getting myself into, and if I was ready to jump into this game with Bishop. Nico taught me enough to survive, but I was about to change everything about Bishop's operation. He was either going to be down and grateful, or I was going to be running a drug empire by myself.

# Good Girlz With Hood Habits

## Bishop

I was down to three days and a wake-up, in this hell hole. Me and Kei were solid, or at least I thought we were. She's been a little distant lately. Every time I called, she was out running errands and couldn't talk to me. I wasn't stressing about it; I knew when I touched down, shit was going to be gravy. I walked off my tier to go holla at the CO that was working on G section that day.

"Yo Williams, what's up with your boy GM?"

"Bankz, don't do that, you know I stopped fucking with him a minute ago."

"Girl, stop, that nigga in love with you."

"That nigga in love with his wife."

"Stop that shit. You know what it is. Anyway, what's up with the two? You got any coming in this week?"

"Yeah, ole girl bringing it in tonight, it'll be broken down and passed out to everyone tomorrow. What do you need Bankz?"

"Just give me a sack."

"Bet, text the numbers tonight."

# Good Girlz With Hood Habits

Williams was cool. She started out green as hell, but GM opened her ass up, and she was making moves on her own now since GM got some time with the feds. These last two months and some change were hectic, to say the least. I was tying up loose ends here and preparing for my life uptown. My nigga Sin was holding shit down for me, but the lil niggas I had on payroll was fucking up. Money was coming up short, the product was missing, and these little niggas was partying more than hustling. They didn't know I was coming home, and I wanted to keep it that way. If shit didn't get better, all their asses were dead.

*Four days later.........*

I walked in the courtroom looking for Kei, but she wasn't anywhere to be found. I hadn't talked to her ass in four days. Four fucking days she's been ignoring me. Soon as these fuckers release me; I was going straight to her house; I was sick of her shit. Court lasted two hours, these motherfuckers didn't want me to leave this hell hole for nothing. But my lawyer was on her shit. At the end of the trial, I was found not guilty and wasn't on any papers. It took them all damn day to discharge

my ass. I walked out of BCDC, a free man and nowhere to go. As

I walked out of the gate, a black Range Rover pulled up, the

window rolled down, and guess who was behind the fucking

wheel…. My baby, Kei!

"Get in Bishop."

"Girl, who truck is this? Where is your car?"

"Can you get in and I'll tell you damn?"

"Girl, who are you talking to?"

She smiled, and I had to laugh; this girl was going to give

me a run for my money. I got in the truck, and Kei reached over

and kissed me, it was a small peck, but it felt like heaven on

earth.

"So, who truck is this woman?"

"Bishop, it's yours. Open the glove compartment. The title is in

there."

I know this girl didn't go buy me a damn truck.

"Kei, you didn't have to do this, and what's all these papers?"

"The top copies are for the truck and the ones right here are for your condo. I didn't think you wanted to come straight to live with me. I know you need your space."

"Kei, I'm going home with you girl, or you coming to live with me in this condo. Now where the fuck you get all this money from?"

Kei' broke down everything about her that I didn't know. Who her dad was, how she was related to the CO Williams, and some shit about my organization?

"Kei, what the fuck you mean you fired my whole team?"

"They were lazy, unappreciative, and lacked work ethic."

"Say less Kei, if you saw that shit, then it needed to be done."

"I'm glad you say that because I also got you a new connect."

"Wait a damn minute, Kei' and I don't want you to take this the wrong way, but what the fuck is you doing? I get it your pops was in this game for years, and I respect that you know some of it, but on some real shit Kei' you don't know shit about connects and this coke shit."

# Good Girlz With Hood Habits

She didn't say anything, just drove and turned the radio up. I was pissed, like don't get me wrong I was grateful for everything Kei was doing, but I'm a fucking man, and this was my lane, not hers. We pulled up to a small townhouse in Dutch Village. I knew this wasn't her house; I had seen pictures and knew her address. When we walked in, I saw my niggas Dam and Kris along with the lil nigga Reggie. Now Dam and Kris were getting big money out in these streets. They used to run with the nigga Nico before he died. I had no idea why we were here or how Kei' knew these niggas, but I was on high alert, nigga wasn't home for 24 hours; I will be damn if my ass was going end up dead because of Kei's ass.

"Yo, my G, what y'all niggas doing here?" I asked Dam, who was the first to speak.

"What's up, Bankz, baby sis came to us for some weight about a month back. Cashed out and been making big moves."

"Oh really," I side-eyed Kei. This shit was a little fishy if you ask me. "What kind of moves is she making?"

# Good Girlz With Hood Habits

Kei started walking to the back of the house; the way this house was set up, the kitchen was the first thing you walked into, then the living room. Kei walked to a closet and pulled out a duffle bag.

"I don't want you to think I'm overstepping, but your organization was weak, and your product was stepped on. Dam and Kris are my big brothers, they had some pure shit, so I hollered at them. The money you gave me that night when you damn near killed a man for dancing with me, I put it with some of my money and bought 15 keys'. Dam said he'll give you 15 a month for 16 a piece. You just gotta get a new crew."

"Are you serious right now? Let me get this straight; you took the money I gave you then added more of your own money, brought 15 keys of coke, fired my crew, and started a damn drug factory in this townhouse in a matter of three months?"

"Yeah, sounds about right, you mad?"

"Nah shorty, how can I be mad at you? Shit, I thought I was coming home to upgrade you, and your ass made me feel like that chic from 'Pretty Woman.' Do your thing, boss lady."

# Good Girlz With Hood Habits

"Good, I'm glad you're okay with it all, here this is for you."

"What's this?"

"It's your part of the profits we made this month."

"Kei, you crazy girl, damn a nigga going love you forever."

"Love me? You love me, Bishop?"

"Something like that, let's get out of here."

I wanted to get Kei to myself. I was ready to shoot the club up if you get what I'm saying. We drove to my new condo; it was a ducked off spot in Cockeysville, Maryland. Kei put the basic's in here but left the decorating for me to do. She knew my favorite colors were blue and orange, so she did my bedroom and bathroom in those colors. My living room just had this oversized tan sectional with burnt orange, toffee, and brown pillows. Everything else was bare. Kei was sitting in the middle of my king size bed when I got out of the shower. She seemed nervous, hell I was too. Yeah, we communicated well on the phone and had a wild ass vibe, but now we were here about to take this to another level. One I have never been too. She crawled to the edge of the bed and put her arms around my neck. Her soft lips touched mine, and I was stuck. They were so soft.

"Kei, I need to tell you something."

"Oh gosh, do you have some type of disease or on the DL or something? Shit, I knew you were too good to be true. Shit, shit, shit," she rambled on like I wasn't even in the room.

"Kei shut the hell up, no, it's nothing like that. It's just I never did this before."

"What do you mean? Like never been in a relationship."

"No, well yeah, that part too, but I never had sex."

"Bishop, stop fucking lying."

"I'm serious, I've only caught head from bitches, never put my dick in one."

"For real, so I'm about to pop your cherry," she laughed.

"You got jokes. I'm for real Kei, if I'm not doing something right, just let me know ard?"

"I got you bae, but to be 100 with you, I've only had sex with one person in my entire life, so we'll be learning each other as we go."

# Good Girlz With Hood Habits

"I dig you, Kei, like for real you the one for me." I kissed her again, this time deeper and with more passion. Kei wrapped her hands around my neck, and I put her legs around my waist. Walking to the side of the bed with her body wrapped around mine, I never broke our kiss. Kei took her left hand and removed my towel and reached for my dick. She stopped kissing me when she found what she was looking for.

"Bishop, what is that?"

"My dick, girl."

"No, that's another arm. What I'm supposed to do with that big ass thing?"

"Now you see why I never fucked, having a big dick is a gift and a curse." She slid down my body and sat back on the bed. Just to let y'all know, I was blessed and cursed with a 13-inch dick. A big black thick dick that caused more trouble than anything. Looking up at me, Kei came back over to me and started stroking my shit.

"Bishop, until I get used to your size, I have to be in control here. Lay down," she said.

# Good Girlz With Hood Habits

I did what I was fucking told. Crawling in between my legs, Kei started rubbing my thighs, moving up to my shaft. Lowering her head, Kei put her warm wet mouth around my dick. Licking the sides and getting the head of my shit wet, Kei put my whole dick in her mouth. Like all 13 inches, was in Kei's mouth, and she didn't gag. She started humming on my dick and playing with my balls at the same time. At that point, I knew I was forever her bitch. She had my toes throwing up gang signs. I know I was moaning like a bitch. The shit was feeling so good. "Kei girl, you gotta stop. I'm about to cum." She didn't listen; I said it two times and before I could say it again, I was cumin down the back of Kei's throat. And this bitch didn't stop. No, like for real, she snatched my soul. She got off the bed and told me to come here. I scooted to the bottom of the bed and waited for her next instructions.

"Grab my breast Bishop," I did. "Put this one in your mouth," I did.

"Play with my nipple while you suck on this one. Yesses, that's right." She let out a low moan.

# Good Girlz With Hood Habits

I took my other hand and slid it in between her legs. Her pussy was so wet. While her titty was still in mouth, I stuck two fingers in her pussy; she was tight and wet. The more I did with my tongue on her titty, the faster she was bucking on my finger. It was driving me crazy; I needed to taste her. I removed my fingers and tossed her ass on the bed. Lifting her legs up, I put my headfirst in her shit. I never ate pussy before, but Kei shit was like a pink frozen cup on a summer day. I started by licking and sucking on her clit, then put two fingers back in her pussy. I had her cumin in a matter of minutes, just like she did me. She came in my mouth two times. I could have died happy right then and there. Exhausted, we both laid down on the bed, just breathing heavily. My dick was hard again, and I was ready to feel Kei.

"Kei, you good?"

"Yeah, Bish, I'm good. You good?"

"Nah, not yet come here."

# Good Girlz With Hood Habits

She turned to face me; I kissed her again. I could never get enough of her lips; they were so soft. I lifted myself up and got in between her. "Let me know if I hurt you." She shook her head.

I played with her pussy a little bit before I started inching inside of my heaven on earth. I knew Kei' was the one for me before I even held her hand. But now feeling the inside of her had me ready to marry her ass.

"Ouuuu Bish, shit that feels so good, do that again," Kei' moaned in my ear. I had to focus on something other than her, or I was going bust in 2.5 seconds. Even her sex faces were sexy as a motherfucker. "Go deeper, Bish."

Now, why would she say that? I straight went savage on her pussy. Had her cumin, screaming, trying to climb the walls, and kill me all at the same time. We fucked all night until the early morning.

"Marry me, Kei," I said as we laid in the aftermath.

"You serious, Bishop?"

"Yeah, you it for me. Let's do it today."

# Good Girlz With Hood Habits

"Bishop, I'll marry you right now, but I want you to be sure this is your heart talking and not your dick."

"Girl, I knew I wanted to marry you the day I first met you."

She laughed, "Bishop, I'll marry you under one condition."

With that, I looked at her with a raised eyebrow.

"We wait a year before we tell anyone, and then we have a big ceremony."

"Why can't we tell nobody?"

"I want us to enjoy each other without other people's opinions."

"You haven't been wrong so far, baby girl, so I'm following your lead. But we are getting married today. Now get over here and suck me up like I like it." She didn't hesitate to put my dick in her mouth. Damn, I love this girl.

# Good Girlz With Hood Habits

## Kei'sha

Now all y'all judgmental people can kiss my ass. Yes, I did some risky shit for my nigga, but hell, I put us in a better position to win in life and upgraded my nigga. How many of you hoes can say that? Bishop was that nigga before, I just elevated him a little, and in return, he gave me his last name. That's right; I'm married now. Tiff and Sin were our witnesses; no one else knew, and I was serious about that one -year condition with Bishop. The wedding was short and sweet.

As we were walking out of the courthouse, gunshots started going off. Bishop used his body to cover mine. The shooting got closer and closer to us. "Kei, stay low, and get back in the building." "Fuck no, I'm not leaving you out here, come in with me." Bishop must have lost his mind if he thought I was leaving him out here naked. He didn't have a gun on him, and neither did Sin. As soon as he was about to say something, a bullet hit him in his back.

# Good Girlz With Hood Habits

"OMG Bishop, Bishop, get up, baby. Please get up." As I was screaming and crying, I noticed a figure getting close to me. I looked up, and it was crazy ass, Eric.

"You stupid bitch I could have given you the world, and you went and married this trash."

"Eric, what are you doing here? You shot my husband!" I screamed.

"Oh, shut up, he's not dead, but he will be if you don't get your ass in this car now."

"I'm not going anywhere with you, you crazy bastard."

He shot Bishop in his leg.

"Next time I'm going shoot him in his head. Now let's go Bitch!"

I looked at Bishop briefly and got up with tears in my eyes as Eric pulled my hair and forced me into his car.

"I'm going to show you I am the man you need, but first, I need you relaxed for this flight."

"Flight, where are you taking me, Eric?"

"Away from here."

# Good Girlz With Hood Habits

He stabbed me with a syringe, and within a matter of seconds, I was out cold.

# Good Girlz With Hood Habits

## Bishop

"Sir, I need you to get back in the bed; you cannot leave this hospital. Do you realize you've been shot several times?"

"With all due respect, lady, I know that, but I gotta find my wife!" I didn't mean to scream at the little white bitch, but I needed her to understand I was nothing without my wife.

Kei' told me about that crazy nigga Eric but I never even thought this shit would happen. Right when I was about to zap again, Sin and Tiff walked in. "Yall find her?"

"Yeah, bro, we found her, but you are not going to like where she's at."

"Sin, don't play with me, where the fuck is my wife?"

"Bro, he took her to Cuba."

"Cuba, what the fuck!" I screamed before I passed out. My damn wife was gone.

To be continued.

**Welcome to the T.E.A.M**

# Good Girlz With Hood Habits

Eisha

So, you're going hear a lot of bull shit about me, and it's cool, believe all that shit. They call me Eisha. Eisha Maye Knicks is my government. Up until I was 12, I lived a good life; I had my mother and father and two little sisters. We lived in Baltimore but had an apartment in Brooklyn because that's where my father's family was from. Anyway, one day my mom, dad, and little sister were in a car accident that took their life. Damn near my whole family was dead; in a matter of minutes, my childhood was stripped from me. My uncle moved my last surviving sister and me upstate with him and his family. At first, it was cool, but it was eight of us living in a four-bedroom house, six females and two males. Money was tight, I mean, we never went without, but I was used to getting my way and whatever I wanted.

My uncle had four kids; Ebony was the oldest, we were really cool at first, but I slipped and tried to fuck her middle school crush, her first boyfriend, and tried to fuck her baby daddy. Listen before you judge me fuck off. I used men and sex

Page 153

to get what I wanted. No one ever molested me, I didn't feel

unloved, and I had a pretty decent childhood even after my

parents died. I just like dick and money, and if I could use one to

get the other, then why the fuck not? My first boyfriend

Dominick taught me how to hustle; he always wanted us to be

on some Bonnie and Clyde shit. Don't get wrong, I loved Nic, but

I was more in love with money.

When I turned 18, I moved back to Baltimore and got

me an apartment in Fells Point. My parents left me a $50k life

insurance policy that I was given once I turned 18. My little

sister got the same amount when she turned 18 as well. When I

moved back to Baltimore, I started dancing at a strip club. I

worked there on Saturdays and Sundays and went job searching

during the week. One of my regular customers at the club told

me his job was hiring. Come to find out he worked as a Sgt. at

Baltimore Center Detention Center. I went to the HR place at

The Plaza and took this long-ass four-hour test. It took about six

months after taking the test to hear anything back, but I got hired. Working there was one of the best and worst things I've done in my life.

I got caught up in some jailhouse soap opera bull shit. I became the plug and was fucking several niggas in this dirty ass jail. But my bank account was fat, and my daughter was well taken care of. My daughter was a product of me and Nic's; he didn't know about her, he thought I got an abortion, but I didn't. I sent her to live with my Aunt Faith and forged Nic's signature relinquishing his rights as her father. Nic turned out to be a real bitch over the years. I mean, I did fuck his little brother, but we weren't together, so it shouldn't matter. His little brother got killed a few years back; if he hadn't, I would have been with him. He was the one I was in love with, the one that was able to tame me. I swear Nic was the one that killed him, but it went down as an unsolved murder.

After that, me and Nic maintained a working relationship and would fuck from time to time. I got pregnant a few times by him, and each time I got rid of the baby but the last one, I was too far along when I found out, so I kept her.

# Good Girlz With Hood Habits

Charity Hope Knicks was my whole heart. I just couldn't give her love like I knew she needed, so my aunt took care of her, but I made sure she had everything she wanted or needed. Anyway, I just came here to introduce myself, don't worry, you'll read more about me in the next book, but for now, go ahead and read these motherfuckers talk big shit about ya girl. I'll be back later.

# Good Girlz With Hood Habits

Dominic

Eisha was a dumb bitch, that fucked me and my little brother for four years straight, then she became a stripper. Eisha was my bitch back in the day, I thought at once I loved her. She was fine as hell, and about her money. We used to get money together, setting niggas up and selling weed. I begged her not to go strip; shit, I was willing to take all the risk and provide for her trifling ass. But the bitch started fucking my brother when I caught a six-month bid. In my mind, she would always be a hoe. I didn't care what she was doing now; she could be President of the United States. She was a hoe in my book. Hell, I know at least ten niggas she fucked while she was working down Norma's. She thought she was so slick like I didn't know she was fucking Ti' ass and was working with Redz. I knew all that shit. What her dumb ass didn't know was me, and Redz was working her ass for cheap labor and a good lay.

Fucking her used to be fun, but now the bitch was getting too messy and becoming a liability. Because of her, I had to kill my little brother and was going to have to put a hit out on my connect cause both their ass was stealing from me. She

thought I wanted her to keep them bastard ass babies she kept

carrying; truth be told, I didn't think none of them was mine. I

can't lie; she's a good worker, did everything I asked her to do,

but she was loose and untrustworthy, so eventually, I was going

to have to put some money on her head.

By the way, my name is Dominic, I run the south side of

BCDC. Being the hall man for D-section allows me to move

freely throughout the jail. Eisha wasn't my only bitch in this jail,

either. I was messing with this other CO name Sawyer; she was

a Sgt. for the juveniles over in the annex building. Shorty was

tech for real. Never heard any bad things about her; she had a

10-year son and a BS degree in Criminal Justice. Baby girl

wouldn't break the law for anything, no matter how slick my

talk was or how much money I sent her. The only thing she was

willing to do was to bring me food and let me talk to my little

sister that was housed with the juveniles.

# Good Girlz With Hood Habits

"Yo, Biscuit, you seen Ant bitch ass?" I hollered at my boy, Biscuit. Biscuit was like my General; if you had a problem or needed something and couldn't get to me, you went to Biscuit.

"Yeah that nigga on G with Gold Mouth and them, you know Ofc. Green on the 40 so that shit wide open."

"Word! Oh shit, I'm about to head up there; you got them numbers for me."

"Yeah, it's seven dots right here."

"Cool, y'all good on product? If not, holla at Beast."

"Ard bet, where you going, my nigga? Up on G?"

"Yeah dummy, one."

"One. Hit the bike when you get up there, love you dummy."

"Love you two, dummy."

Ofc. Green was one of Redz baby mommas, so she let us shag when she was on the 40.

"Hey, Green."

"Hey Nick, where you going, down G?"

"And you know it, is your man down there?"

"No, he in medical right now; you want me to tell him to come down there."

"Yeah, tell him I'll be in Archie cell. Yo, Green."

"Yeah Nick?"

"What's up with that new Sgt Williams? She got any 'Drake' in her?"

"Fuck no, her ass is green as shit, a little slow if you ask me. But you know Barney wants your ass."

"Man, fuck no, I'm not fucking with her ass, she another jailhouse hoe. Nah, I'm good. But look, let me get down here before shift change. Who is working down there anyway?"

"Your girl Barney," she laughed and walked away.

I hated that lady with a passion; she was a big old freak. Her pussy was trash, and I do mean garbage! She was another one that fucked my whole jail click. I walked past F-section and gave a few "what's up's" to some of my goons and customers. I knew Redz was probably in medical chopping it up with his first baby momma Knowles. According to him, that was his only baby momma in the jail; the other three had to get tested first before

# Good Girlz With Hood Habits

he claimed any of them. Out of all of them, Knowles was the realist; she was average looking but down for her man.

Green was high yellow with that good Indian hair, the shit that bitches spend whole checks on with a phat ass. Green was just too naive for me. Shorty was 27 with five kids; one was 15, that's too many raw dicks going in that pussy for me. But she was mad cool and a sweetheart. Redz other baby momma, Washington was a mean bitch, I still don't know how he pulled her.

Getting back to my money stroll, that nigga Ant still had my bike from when I went on lock up last month, and from what I hear, he was trying to keep the shit. Ant was a part of the organization I was in called the BGF; some people confused us with a gang, but umm nah, I wouldn't say it was a gang more like a family that sometimes had to use violence to get people to see things our way. Anyway, that's the only reason that nigga Ant was still walking right now, but I was going to holla at Redz so his pill-popping ass can get sanction. I was tired of this bull shit.

"Yo, you niggas up here bull shitting and the niggas over the

Northside getting all this fucking money, fuck is y'all doing?"

"Nic, chill, we got that bitch Smith over J section, so shit open

till three, besides Archie and Gold Mouth in the damn room

fucking Barney. We are looking out," the nigga Savage said.

"Man, you niggas is crazy. It's the middle of the day, we got

product to sell, and y'all niggas worried about a fucking orgy

with Barney freak ass. I'm out! You niggas geeking."

I left their dumb ass and headed back to my section. I

needed to really holla at Redz before shift change; I heard a

shake down was supposed to be going down soon. Walking back

through the 40, I saw Eisha freak ass walking some guys through

medical; we didn't acknowledge each other, just a head nod,

and kept it moving. Redz was walking my way when I turned to

go down the long hallway.

"What's good dummy," Redz said as he was walking down the

hall.

"Ant?" I asked.

"Green light," Redz responded.

# Good Girlz With Hood Habits

"Shake down?" I questioned.

"Drain it," Redz told me.

"One!" I said, and walked away.

That was the extent of our conversation, always never too much, just enough so we could know what was going on. If you don't speak jail, let me break it down for you. Redz just gave the okay to sanction Ant bitch ass; I informed him of the upcoming shake down and was instructed to dump the trap cell. Got it? Good. Moving on. Time to get some pussy.

Walking through the long hallway, I had to sneak past 46 cuz that's where the Sgt and Lt's be, and depending on who was on duty, I might get caught up. Through the north side stairwell was post 11, post 11 was a grill that blocked jumping J and killer K, which were supposedly the worst sections in the jail. I don't believe it, but whatever. Thank god post 11 was wide open. I walked right on J section and kissed the love of my life right in her mouth. Yes, I was married, no this wasn't my wife, but it was the next best thing.

# Good Girlz With Hood Habits

Larissa Syed had my heart. I met her two years ago when I was across the street in the Jail Industries Building; she was 19 when I met her and new to corrections. The JI Building is where the working men usually sleep, it has five dorms, and most of the CO's that work over here are on their way to retirement. So, to have a young ass fine CO in this building was a rarity. At the time, she was in love with the father of her twins, so she wasn't hearing any of the bull shit I was talking about, but we became best of fucking friends doing my eight months there. By the time I got out, her and her baby father were over, and me and the wife were living in separate houses. So, we became a couple well, not out in the open, but every night, I laid my head on her breast, whether her apartment or my mom's house didn't matter. That girl was crazy about me, but I broke her heart when I moved to PA with my wife. When I got locked up this last time, I called her instead of my wife or mother. She would give her last breathe for me, and I just played and dogged her every time. I don't know why she still takes my damn phone calls.

# Good Girlz With Hood Habits

"Ummmmm, hey bae, what took you so long to get down here?"

"Just making my rounds and getting this paper for real. What you miss a nigga or something?"

"Nah, Puppy Nuts, I just want my damn money." We both laughed; now I would give her my last dollar because she never asked for any fucking thing.

Walking to the back of the tier, we went to the vacant cell where all the work was held. No one knew that the floorboard and ceiling opened up. I found out about this spot a few months ago when me and Syed were fucking, J section was her permanent post, so she was able to deadline this cell so no one would be housed in here. I had a trap cell upstairs on D section that niggas knew about, but this cell had over 50 thousand dollars of work in it and five stacks of cash on hand. Eisha didn't even know that I knew Syed, but Syed knew about Eisha because we had that type of relationship, and Syed knew Eisha was just for financial purposes only.

"What you taking today?"

"Just the buks and 4oz of exotic. Put these three numbers on my rush card, give momma these two and pay the twins tuition with these. Oh, take that five out of here too."

"Ard, the buks in the sink, exotic top bunk," she pointed to the bed. "I gotta take mommy to work in the morning, so I'll load her cards. You paid the twins tuition up for the year Nic; they don't need anything else. What should I do with the five?

"It's yours, happy birthday, dirty. You thought I forgot, didn't you?"

"No, I knew you would remember, thanks, Puppy Nuts."

"Oh man, you know I'm Dog Balls, and you're Puppy Nuts."

"Whatever man, you chilling down here or nah."

"Nah bae, I gotta get back over to the south side before shift change."

"So, wait, I can't get none on my birthday?"

"See there you go, no you can't I gotta make moves," I told her as I was putting the weed in my dip.

# Good Girlz With Hood Habits

Syed didn't have a man uptown. I knew that for a fact because my other little sister Deja was living with her. So, she knew not to bring no niggas in my house. Yeah, it was my house cause I paid the damn bills. Syed lived in a 3-bedroom townhouse on Loch Raven around the corner from my mother. Her rent was like $900, her twins Tristan and Tion, went to a private school not too far from her house. All she did was work, go to school, and be a mom. I loved that about her; she was a good girl in every sense of the words.

"Well, can I at least get a piece of cake for my birthday?"

"Larissa! I just gave you over $8000 you can buy your own damn...."

Before I could finish my sentence off, she had my dick in her mouth

"Rissssss, what are you doing?"

"I'm getting my damn cake!"

I was in complete shock y'all. Syed never, and I do mean never sucked my dick before. Never in all the years, I've known her. It was something I've learned to live without.

# Good Girlz With Hood Habits

"Damn bae, ouch wait bae move your teeth, yeah, that's it. Now

spit on it ummm mmmm oh shit, do that thing again," she

twirled her tongue around the tip of my dick; that shit felt good.

I had to coach her for the first couple minutes, but she learned

fast; five minutes later, I was about to bust.

"Riss, chill, I'm about to cum." I tried pulling away from her, but

she sucked me in harder, forcing me to do nothing else but

come in her mouth, and she swallowed, all of it no spitting.

Damn, she fucked my head up with that. I had to come back

strong. I punished her guts for the rest of her shift. By 3:05,

when her relief was coming down the hall, we were rushing to

clean things up and put our lie in order.

Shit Eisha was working 2nd shift, fuck she was doing

here on her day off anyway, then to work a double at that? She

must be making some moves today. When she saw me, she

gave me this weird look like what the fuck you doing down

here?

"Hey, Ofc Syed, everybody locked in?"

# Good Girlz With Hood Habits

"Yeah and the count is 86; the breakdown is right there on the table."

"What about that inmate, is he in this section?"

"Ummm no, he had to bring down new mop heads from the 40. I'm escorting him back to the south building on my way out. Anything else you need?"

"No thanks, Syed, enjoy the rest of your day."

I knew Syed was mad as shit that Eisha was questioning her, but she would never show it. That's a true ride or die for real. I got back to my cell and had a missed call from my man's Beast. Word on the street was the nigga Moshi was coming for my head and sending someone in to knock me off my square. Never going to fucking happen! I was god in this jail, especially since that mixed breed Bishop ass was finally out this mother fucker. He could send God and his 12 disciples at me, and I still would come out on top. Fuck I look like being worried about another nigga? I drag my nuts around this bitch. They ain't birth a nigga yet that can stop me. Ya, dig? Anyway, my time is up; I be back until then read about the nigga that's supposed to

come and knock me off my square. I'm outie 5000.

# Good Girlz With Hood Habits

Trevor

I met Eisha through my children's mother Eboni, when Eisha was like 19 or something. Eboni was from New York; I met her on Spring Break in Miami; she was a junior at Long Island University and that year was my last year at Morgan State University. When we first started talking, it was really hard because she lived in NYC, and I was from the 410, but once I graduated, I would spend all my time upstate with her. Eisha is Eboni's cousin. Eisha lived in Baltimore too, so sometimes we would catch the train upstate together. Eisha has always been cool towards me besides the times she tried to fuck me, but over the years, she learned that I was a one-woman man. I guess it didn't hurt that Eboni fucked her up the summer of 06 for trying to fuck me at her graduation cookout. We found out shortly after the fight Eboni was pregnant with our first set of twins.

Tony and Erin were born on September 19, 2007. That changed a lot in our life. For starters, Eboni moved with me in my one-bedroom apartment at The Commons of White Marsh in White Marsh, Maryland. I worked at BG&E at the time as an engineer. When the twins turned one, Eboni was pregnant again. This time a little girl. Hazel-Marie, born on May 13th, 2009, was a true daddy's girl and a lil fat momma. So here we were, two adults, three kids under three living in a one-bedroom apartment. Something had to give. Eboni started working at The Spot hair salon as a shampoo girl until she could find a job in her field, which was anthropology. Two years later, she was still trying to find herself; this time, she was enrolled at Coppin State University for Criminal Justice. Tony had asthma, Erin went to private school, and Hazel wore glasses. To top it off, our fourth child came. Arianna -Faith was born June 8th, 2011. Four kids, one income, and now in a three-bedroom townhouse, was enough to drive any man to drink.

*August 2012......*

I walked in the house I shared with my kid's mom with a stack full of bills and Eboni's recent credit card statement. Lord, that woman could shop, our limit was $6,500, and I swear as soon as I could pay it off, she was back at the mall charging

some more unnecessary shit that neither the kids nor we

needed. I just shook my head and greeted my woman of eight

years.

"Hey, Ma."

"Hey, baby, how was your day?"

Eboni was at the stove trying to cook. I love Eboni with

all my heart, but she couldn't cook to save her damn life; that's

where most of our money went beside the mall.  It was either

Mo's or fucking Stokos.

"Baby, did you have to spend $500 in Towson? What in the hell

did you buy? Did you use the coupon app?"

"Yes, I did, Mr. Ballard. First Tony needed new shoes, Erin

needed uniforms, Ari needed underclothes, and I had to pay for

Hazel's glasses because our insurance wouldn't pay for the

frames she wanted, and coupons are so tacky."

"I can bet you those frames were Ray Bands and too much for a

damn three almost four-year-old."

# Good Girlz With Hood Habits

She was standing at the stove with some Victoria Secret Pink sweatpants and a half shirt with a pink heart on it. While she was talking, I couldn't help but notice how good she looked. I can't lie after eight years and four babies, my shorty still looked good as fuck! Her booty had grown and so had her titties, she didn't have a flat stomach, but it wasn't a pot belly or anything like that. Her hair was in a ponytail with a bang in the front. It's crazy that no matter how many years or babies, she still had the look of a teenager. On her neck was a necklace with T.E.A.M Ballard on it, each letter stood for one of our kids. Just looking at her made my dick jump. She was everything a man wanted or needed; smart, sexy, silly, and a complete slut when it came to the bedroom. How do you think all the kids came about? I walked up behind her and started playing with her nipples; that was her spot.

"Oh no, you don't, get away from here, I'm trying to cook Snoo." (Snoo was her nickname for me.)

"What stink I'm not doing nothing, just giving you a hug."

By this time, my hand was down the front of her sweatpants.

# Good Girlz With Hood Habits

"Where are the kids?" I asked her.

Breathing heavily, she said, "The twins and fat mamma are at the after-school program, and Ari is with Aunt Faith."

She barely got the words out before I felt her juices running down my hand. I love the feel of my woman. I knew what she needed, what she wanted, how she reacted to every touch, kiss, and move; she was made for me. I lifted her up on the island in the kitchen; she knew when I put her in this position that I wasn't playing any games.

Removing my jacket and shirt, I looked at the clock on the microwave; it read, 4:47 pm. The after-school program got out at six and I needed to be finished by 5:30, so the kids could get picked up on time. With no further delay, I lifted both of Eboni's legs and dove my face into the sweet wetness of the love of my life. I loved eating Eboni's box; for some reason, it always tasted like sunshine.

"Snoo, oh my god, yes, daddy, fuck! Eat this pussy."

# Good Girlz With Hood Habits

Her Caramel skin against my chocolate face was exotic. I stuck one finger inside of her. Her pussy gripped to my finger; I put one more in. "Snoo baby, put me down I got to taste you."

Remember when I said my girl was a slut, well sucking dick was her specialty. She could put my dick and balls in her mouth at the same time without gagging, and that wasn't an easy task because my dick cleared 9inches easily. What started out as me taking control of her turned into me screaming like a little bitch.

"Eboni baby damn, yes, suck that dick, you fucking slut."

"You like that, daddy?"

She started saying something in Spanish before my dick disappeared again. Two minutes later, I was cumming, and Eboni swallowed all my babies.

"Now let me finish cooking, man," Eboni said while I gathered myself.

Her big mistake was turning her back on me and bending down to pull up her pants. BINGO! By the time she got her pants to her knees, my dick was inside of her.

# Good Girlz With Hood Habits

"You thought you were going to just suck daddy dick and not give me none of my pussy, huh?"

She didn't answer; she just threw her hips back on me.

"Oh, you can't talk now?" With every stroke, I tried my hardest to literally 'kill' her pussy.

"Baby, please, oh my god baby, please don't stop, Fuck me Trevor."

And with all my might, I fucked the dog shit out of my woman. At 5:30, I was still knee-deep in my pussy and wasn't stopping any time soon. So, while Eboni was riding my dick, I told her to call Aunt Faith (Eboni's favorite aunt) and ask if she could get the kids for the rest of the night. We fucked the rest of the day away, and by 9 pm, we were tired, sweaty, and hungry. We ended up ordering from Stokos's.

"Ummm Snoo, we need to talk," Eboni said while we were watching an old episode of Martin

"What's up, baby?"

"Well, you remember when I put that application in with the Police Department as a clerk in the records division?"

"Yeah, and I also remember telling you that I didn't want you doing it either, so what's up?"

"Well, bae, I got the job; they called me today to come in to fill out all the paperwork and get my ID."

"Eboni, we've talked about this; I don't want you working right now. I just got a bonus, and we are comfortable, and you don't have to work. Besides, who the hell will watch the kids and take care of this house, huh Eboni?" I said, getting mad as we spoke. Eboni knew I didn't trust just anyone to watch our kids, especially at this young age.

"Well, here's the thing, Auntie retired, so she will watch them, and I would work 9 am-5 pm Monday, Tuesday, Thursday, Friday, and Sunday. So, I could still do everything I normally do around the house. Plus, baby, we need the extra income because ummmmmm well."

Oh, I hated when Eboni stalled; she only did that three times so far in our whole relationship, and each time a kid came about. "Well, what Eboni, I know you're not about to tell me what I think."

# Good Girlz With Hood Habits

She put her head down.

"No, no, no bae, we were so careful, damn I can't believe this.

How far are you?"

With tears in her eyes, she said, "seven weeks but ummmm

baby, that's not all."

I wonder what else could there be, but before I could voice it,

Eboni answered my inner thoughts with.

"It's twins."

If looks could kill, that sweet woman I just made love to

would have been dead. Twins fucking twins, what kind of sperm

did I have? Six fucking kids, who was going to feed them, cloth

them? No, Eboni didn't need a job; what she needed was

fucking birth control! I wanted to scream, jump, run the fuck

away, anything other than this shit! Don't get me wrong, I love

my kids and Eboni, but I made $75,000 a year before taxes. We

had two car notes, rent, insurance on three cars, student loans,

medical co-pays, cable, and a slew of other bills. Eboni brought

home about $1600 a month in added income with her part-time

job at the salon but with four kids that were used for food and clothes.

"SNOO, are you listening...."

Eboni screamed at me. Fuck no, I wasn't listening. I was thinking of a damn escape plan.

"Yes, bae, finish what you were saying."

"Well, the job starts me off with $35,700, but then after the training and 90-day probation, I'll get a salary increase of ten thousand a year."

"That's fine, Eboni, tell them you'll take the job. I'm going hit Mo's really quick for a drink and talk to Moshie. I'll be back in a few."

With that, I got up off the couch and left the house. When I reached the car, Eboni sent me a text. I ignored it. I knew she would cuss my ass out for leaving like that, but I needed to clear my head. I met up with my nigga Moshie at Mo's. He was my homey from down Eager St. We hooked up my first year at St. Francis. It's funny because we came from two different worlds but were closer than brothers. Moshie was half

# Good Girlz With Hood Habits

African and in Africa was damn near a prince. His dad was a big-time drug dealer in the states. Mr. Knight was a cool ass African for real. When my mom couldn't afford new Jordan's or name brand shit like that, Mr. Knight bought it for me. Matter fact, it was him that helped my mom buy me my first car in the 12th grade. I had wanted this used all black 98 BMW 2 door coupe. It was six years old with less than 90000 miles with gold VVS's. The guy was selling it for $4500, and between my mom and my earnings from my part-time job at Shoe City, we only had $3200. Mr. Knight gave us the rest. That was years ago before babies and bills.

Moshi's family helped me out in high school and life. It was Moshi's dad that bought my books and food while I was at MSU. Needless to say, Moshi was all my kids' godfather, and I guess he was going to be the new one's god father too. Moshi gave me the hindsight I needed to take my black ass home and makeup with the wifey and embrace the two new bundles of joys about to enter the Ballard's gang.

"Yo, Eboni is pregnant again," I said, drowning my third shot of patron within 15 minutes.

"So, what that's nothing new, Eboni always pregnant," he laughed.

"Nigga that shit ain't funny, what the fuck I'm do with two more kids?"

"Nigga she pregnant with twins?"

"Yes, asshole, that's what I'm trying to tell you this whole time. What the fuck am I going to do?"

"Shit, first, we need to sell some of that super sperm you got my nigga. How the fuck your none dick having ass get two sets of twins in one lifetime?"

"Yo, I don't know, but I'm ready to pack up and run the fuck away."

"I should smack the shit out of you for that bitch ass shit you just said. What you are going to do is take your black ass back home and pray sis didn't change the locks on your dumb ass, fuck her ass really good, and apologize for being a punk. Might as well marry her ass too because ain't no bitch going to give you any play with six kids," he burst out laughing. "Yo, take your bitch ass home to my god kids before I make them my step kids."

"Eboni don't want your black ass, so I ain't worried. I'm out, one."

We dapped then rolled out. Thanks to that nigga patron, I was feeling nice and wanted to punish Eboni's guts then apologize for being a dick head. Heading home, I made a left on President Street so I could jump on 83 North to get home. I wanted to avoid lights and cops, my dick was jumping, and it needed to be in the mouth of my own personal freak. I sent Eboni a text in Spanish, letting her know to have that thing wet and ready for me. Three minutes later, my phone chimes with a message from Eboni saying, "hurry up daddy, before I start without you." Attached to the message was a picture of Eboni pretty shaved pink pussy soaking wet. I damn near crashed my car. I had to swerve into two different lanes to keep from hitting my shit. When I finally got it under control, no other than Baltimore county's highway patrol pulled me over.

Shit!

This white prick must have smelled the liquor on my breath, he made me get out my car, walk the straight line, recites my alphabet backward, and tell him my first, middle, and last name along with my address. After barely passing those tests, I thought I was done, but ole Charlie just had to do the breathalyzer test. I was two times past the legal drinking limit, that was it, I was going to jail. It took all of three minutes before the cuffs were put on and my rights read. I never got my dick sucked that night. I was booked for reckless endangerment, driving while on a handheld, DUI, and the bitch ass cop gave me a work order for a broken taillight. Just my fucking luck.

# Good Girlz With Hood Habits

Eboni

Hey, world, it's me fertile myrtle. Me and Trevor have been together for about six years now. It wasn't always good between us. Trevor had his ways and was stubborn. He never cheated or disrespected me, but he did do shit like stop talking to me for days at a time but would still be around me. I remember this one time I spilled water on his pants by mistake, and this asshole stopped talking to me for three days, mind you I was six months pregnant at the time. Yeah, we've been through a lot and had a lot of fucking kids. Now with two more on the way, I knew I would have to start telling my Snoo the truth. I wanted to wait until we were married, but with two more kids coming, I knew it was time. Y'all will find out what I was talking about in a little bit, and no, I'm not cheating, damn.

Anyway, that night after I told Snoo about the two new additions to our family, I waited up all night for this nigga to come in here. I knew how it was going to go; he was going eat my soul out my body, I was going to suck the skin of his dick, we'd fuck hard, then he'd apologize for being an ass, make breakfast, and if the kids were here, he would have taken them to school and daycare for me. I knew my man very well. But when my alarm woke me up at 7 am and Snoo wasn't home, I was pissed the fuck off! In all the years we've been together, this nigga never stayed out past two. Where the fuck was he? He better have a pretty good damn reason as to why he never came home or called after getting me all hot and shit. I went to my aunt's house to pick the kids up for school and went home and paced the fucking floor. I called his best friend Moshi to see if he was with him, but he hadn't seen him since last night. So now pissed was turning into worry.

By noon when I hadn't heard anything, I started calling local hospitals; it never dawned on me to call central booking because Snoo never got into trouble, not even a speeding ticket. At 1:02, my phone rang with a collect call from Trevor Ballard at the Baltimore Central Booking and intake center. The love of my life was sitting in jail for a DUI.

# Good Girlz With Hood Habits

Trevor

Calling Eboni was the hardest thing I had to do. When I told her where I was and what the charges were, I could feel a part of my manhood breaking down. I told her to call Moshi and for them to come to bail me out. My bail was set at $25,000, but with a bail bond, I would only need $2,500 but Eboni didn't have pay stubs because she worked under the table at the salon, so Moshi was going to have to pull me out of this jam. I sat in central booking for 23 hours before Eboni and Moshi could get me out. I thanked my brother from another mother and took my wifey home. After the tears of concern were wiped away, Eboni went in on my ass. She wasn't feeling that I might have to do a few months behind bars bullshit.

"Snoo, how could you be so fucking stupid? Drinking and driving, what the fuck, what if someone would have hit your stupid ass. I can't believe you, now what if your ass gotta go to jail, who's going help with all these fucking bills and kids I'm so mad at you right now, ughhhhhh?"

The whole time she was fussing at me, I was inching up behind her slowly with all intent to finish what we had started before I got booked.

"You're right, bae I shouldn't have been drinking and driving, I'm sorry."

I knew if I said it was her fault since I was reading her damn message when I swerved, I wouldn't be getting any of that juicy box and after spending a total of 25 hours and 32 minutes in the booking. I wasn't trying to go to sleep with a dry dick and mad woman. So, I let her say her piece, and while she was telling me how selfish that was, I was rubbing her butt and running my fingers through her hair; it wasn't until my thumb and index finger was pinching her nipples that she stopped talking to see what I was doing.

"Oh, hell no, Trevor Donatello Ballard, you are not getting any tonight no, no, no, no!"

"Girl, shut up, and give me my pussy."

# Good Girlz With Hood Habits

Eboni tried to play like she was tough, but we both knew who the king in this house was. And when I say I want my pussy she knows to can all that damn noise and ride this face.

"No, Snoo."

"Eboni, you're telling me no?"

"Yes, you don't deserve any."

"You're right, what was I thinking? I'm sorry, Stink, come give daddy a kiss."

When she lifted her arms up to hug my neck, I lifted her off the floor and on my shoulders. She must have forgotten I was 100+ pounds, bigger than her, and did 75 push-ups two times a day, and the fact that she had on a damn skirt did nothing but help me. I used my teeth to pull her panties to the side and dug my tongue into her creamy middle.

"Snoo, what are you doing? Omg put me down, oh shit, daddy no, no, no, yes, yes, yes."

I had her trying to climb the wall. I smacked her ass and felt her ass cheeks jiggle on my face. When she was cumming for the second time, I put her down and walked away. Her little

Page 189

ass thought I was done, oh no baby girl; I got something for that

ass. You see, Eboni liked that dominatrix shit, so I went into the

kid's room and got one of their belts.

"Crawl to daddy slowly."

"Yes, daddy!"

"Did I tell you to talk? Get over here and don't say a word."

When she reached my feet, I lifted her face and slightly

smacked it. "When daddy tells you to do something, what are

you supposed to do?"

"Do whatever daddy says."

"Now give me my pussy!

She laid back with her legs pushed back to her head. I got down

and sucked the soul out her pussy.

Smack! "Who's pussy is this?"

"Yours, daddy."

"Say my name, Eboni."

"Snoo!"

I pushed all 9 inches of my dick in her while she

screamed my name, in and out, circle, ramming it all the way in, then taking it out. Eboni's box was so fucking wet and good. She started throwing that big ass back, and I damn near lost it. I loved fucking with the windows open, so I had Eboni open them bitches up. I was definitely in freak mode right now.

"Open them blinds and lift that fucking window!" She did as she was told.

"Now get over here and suck this dick and you better not stop until I tell you too!"

Eboni walked over to me with her toes perfectly manicured, squatted down, and took my whole dick in her mouth. Spitting on my already wet shaft, she sucked the head of my dick like a fucking vacuum cleaner. Licking her juices off of me, she placed her right hand on my balls, while blowing into the tip of my head. That was new, but it felt good. With no hands, Eboni deepthroated my dick like a suction cup; I was moaning like a little bitch. Eboni was trying to make me cum, but I wasn't done with her ass. In a swift motion I lifted Eboni up by her waist and put her in a 69 position, bringing her wet pussy to my mouth again. Fucking her with my tongue, I was making it hard for her to keep my dick in her mouth. When she busted in my mouth, I put her down.

"Didn't I tell you to suck this dick until I said so, you can't handle when I put that fat ass pussy in my mouth can you?" She tried to speak. "Nah, don't talk now, get up and come sit on your dick." When she positioned herself on my lap with my dick inside of her, I placed my hands on the side of her face and said, "Stink, I would never do anything purposely to hurt you or my kids, if this mistake takes me away from y'all, just know that daddy won't be gone long and I'm still going to provide for my family. You understand, Eboni?"

With tears in her eyes, she shook her head yes.

"No, say the words, Eboni."

"Yes, Snoo, I understand."

"Now stop crying and ride daddy dick."

That night Eboni rode me to sleep. She bucked and grind like it was going to be the last time she got to do it. Before cumming I kissed her stomach and asked her to marry me.

# Good Girlz With Hood Habits

## Eboni

I woke up feeling incredible. Although my pussy was swollen, my man was home, the sun was shining, my aunt took the kids for the rest of the week while Snoo and I dealt with this DUI bull shit, and I was getting married. Yep, I was officially becoming a Ballard. Snoo decided that we needed to make it official. I mean, it has been damn near six years, and with six kids, neither one of our asses was going anywhere. Besides, I couldn't handle everything if he had to do jail time as his "baby momma," we told my aunt and Moshi, but that was it. We would wait to see what happens in court before we had a big ceremony, for right now, we were going to the courthouse.

On August 6th, I married the man of my dreams, the father of my children, my lover, my best friend, and my soulmate. Moshi and his girl of the week were our witnesses. Afterward, we went to meet Snoo's lawyer to discuss our options.

# Good Girlz With Hood Habits

Trevor

I married my heart, y'all. I'm mad it took me this long but better late than never, right? Anyway, after our courthouse ceremony, I met with my lawyer. Heather Lopez was one of the best up and coming lawyers in Baltimore. Mr. Knight paid my legal fees as a wedding present. No matter what happened to me, that man was always there to get me through tight spots. Lopez wanted me to take this shit to court, but I could have gotten up to three years, so I took a plea deal. I would do six months of jail time and have to perform 100 hours of community service, but that was it. Because I had four kids and a pregnant wife to deal with, I also got the DA to give me at least 30 days to get my affairs in order before turning myself in.

October 24th, 2012, was the date set to turn myself in. Eboni and I didn't want the kids to know what was going on, so we told them I was going on a business trip for six months. As far as my job, I never took days off or used any of my vacation time, so my boss let me go on an early paternity leave in which I'd still get paid for three months, and then I'd use my vacation

# Good Girlz With Hood Habits

time for eight weeks. That last month would be the only struggle financially. Eboni wanted to take that job with the state to help out more, but this was a high-risk pregnancy, so her doctor wouldn't release her to work in such a hostile environment. Plus, with me gone, I needed her home with my kids.

We had a nice little savings account, so I knew we would be okay. Eboni's Aunt Faith called her cousin Eisha to let her know I was going to be in there, and to look out for me. Eisha was into a lot of shady shit in the jail that Aunt Faith nor Eboni knew about; however, I knew, and I was going holla at her about getting me a phone while I was in there. We found out Eboni was due March 27th. I was hoping for two boys, but either way was fine with me; however, Eboni and I both decided to get fixed after the twins were born. Six was enough for me.

# Good Girlz With Hood Habits

Eboni

*October 24$^{th}$.........*

The day Snoo had to turn himself in was the worst day of my life. I was a wreck! I stayed up all night the night before and barely ate anything that whole day. I tried to put on a brave face, but deep inside, I was dying. I know it's only six months, but that man meant everything to me, and I wasn't sure how this family would make it without him. I called Eisha's trifling ass just to get clarity on how jail was and what Snoo was in for, but that bitch wasn't know damn help. I guess she never got over the fact that I beat her ass for trying to fuck Snoo at my graduation party. Freak ass bitch!

"Eisha, make sure you look out for my husband."

"Eboni, get the fuck off my phone with that bull shit. Trevor is a grown-ass man and can take care of himself."

"Well, damn bitch fuck you too."

"You better hope I don't fuck that fine ass man of yours!"

"And you better hope I don't kill your bitch ass this time!"

# Good Girlz With Hood Habits

With that, I hung up on her bitch ass. I guess too many years have passed without me whipping her ass. However, if she keeps talking out the side of her neck, I'll have to come out of retirement. Fuck that bitch.

Ring ring ring

"How are you holding up, sis?"

"Moshi, how the fuck you think I'm holding up? I want my man, the kids are gone, and I'm in this fucking house by myself pregnant with nothing to do! That's how I'm holding up damnit!"

"Yo, chill E damn! Open the door."

I walked to the door, and Moshi and Mr. Knight stood there with their hands filled with bags.

"Hi, Poppa Knight, what are you doing here?"

"Waiting for you to invite me in Lady E."

"Oh, I'm sorry come in."

When they walked in, four other guys walked in behind them with bags from True Religion, Ralph Lauren, DTLR, Nordstrom, Saks, Gap Kids, Crazy 8, and Lucky Jeans.

"What's all this stuff?"

"Well, Lady E, these are for you, and the bags these gentlemen are carrying are for my grandkids, and those are for Erin and Tony."

"What's for the twins?"

Just then, Moshi came back to the house, pushing two brand new kids motorized BWM cars with Erin and Tony on the plates. All I could do was cry, my twins birthday was the 19th of September, and because of all this mess with Snoo, we really didn't do much besides cake, ice cream, and a few gifts. But of course, their God Father and Poppa Knight took care of everything and got them everything we hadn't and much more.

"Eboni, you're not by yourself. We're not just Trevor's family, and you know that. Lock up the house and come stay at the Knights house."

"But...."

"But nothing, let's go, Eboni."

When Poppa Knight calls me by my real name, I know he is serious. Putting all the bags away and locking up, I got in the car. I was surprised when Mr. Knight handed me his Galaxy

5 phone.

"Hello."

"Hey, baby girl, you miss daddy?"

The waterworks just started falling, "Snoo, baby, I miss you so

much."

"Eboni, it's only been a day damn," he chuckled.

"Don't laugh at me negro, how are you holding up?"

"I'm good, baby girl, listen I want you to go enjoy yourself,

Poppa Knight, and I have agreed that from now on you, and the

kids will stay with him and Momma Knight until I get uptown.

Mooch will look after the house, and Pedro will take the kids to

school and pick them up."

"Snoo, I don't want to be a bother, and the Knight's house is all

the way in DC, that's too far of a commute bae."

"Eboni, do what I say, it's only 45 minutes away. I need you to

worry about the twins and having that box wet when I get

home. Got it?"

"Okay, Snoo, I'll stay."

"That's my girl. I love you to the moon."

"And back, Snoo."

"Ard, I'm gone. I'll try to call y'all again later. One!"

I gave Poppa Knight his phone back and silently cried myself to sleep in the back of his car. This was going be a long six months

# Good Girlz With Hood Habits

## Trevor

When I hung up the phone, I set out to do the mission at hand. There was a reason Eboni was going to stay at the Knights house. I was about to embark on a new life, and it wasn't just sitting in jail for six months. Remember I told you Mr. Knight was like a king over in Africa? Well, he was sort of. Fucking Knight was a platinum-selling African singer in the late 70's early 80's. He came to the United States hoping to get an American record deal and become an international recording singer. While here, he met and fell in love with a go-go dancer at Studio 54. Mrs. Knight was a bad redbone back in the day. She had a model body and was smart but was a true 70's /80's party girl with no intentions of settling down and being anyone's wife, no matter how rich they were. Mr. Knight spent hundreds of thousands of dollars flying her all over the country, buying her the finest clothes and the biggest diamonds. Yet she still wouldn't settle down and stay away from the party scene. Condoms weren't really used back then, so when she got pregnant, Mr. Knight just knew he had her. Unfortunately, it wasn't until their third and final child, a little boy, that she

decided to marry Mr. Knight. After that, Mr. Knight moved his

family to Washington, DC. When it became apparent that he

wasn't getting an American record deal, Mr. Knight used his

resources and took to the drug trade.

Being a part of the party scene allowed Mrs. Knight to

help her husband create contacts in high places. With coke

being the biggest thing to hit the streets, Mr. Knight took full

advantage of the Coca Plants his village in Africa grew and his

private plane. Yeah, that nigga became a kingpin in no time.

Years later, Mr. Knight is no longer in charge of the

import/export aspect of the business, Moshi is. Mr. Knight

cleaned the family's money by opening two-night clubs, a small

car dealership, four daycare centers, a beauty salon, and a

barbershop. The Knight's owned a fleet of cars, six homes in the

tri-state area, two planes, and a sprinter bus. Luxury was never

a problem. When Moshi took over the business, he added a few

new avenues for the drug business. Five years ago, Moshi got

booked and convicted for some bullshit and had to do 18

months at BCDC. While there, he made contacts with the swingers and shakers of the jail. He got his dad to make some moves, and now the Knight family was in charge of all contraband moving in and out of the central region of Maryland correctional facilities.

As much as he was loved, he was hated too. Moshi was being undercut in prices by Eisha and this nigga named Redz, causing the Knights to lose 30% of their profits. As cool as Eisha was, Moshi and Mr. Knight were my family. So, when Mr. Knight asked me to help him, there wasn't a question in my mind to do it. My job was to get in Eisha's head and get her to relinquish control over to me so I can give the business back to the Knight family. We all know how females worked, so we came up with the idea that I'd fuck her silly and play with her mind to get what was needed. Easier said than done, though.

First, Eboni couldn't find out, or that was my ass. Second, I didn't know where in the jail she worked, what section, or what shift. So, I had to go fishing. I saw my man's Naheem on B-section when I was coming in. Lil nigga was cool for real. He had a baby by Eboni's best friend Leah, so we would

see each other at birthday parties and any sleepover drop off.

He had the hook up on almost everything from weed to pills

even down to clothes; he was like a one-stop-shop. We never

really did any business together because I was always on the

straight and narrow. I did, however, buy a few pairs of True

Religion jeans from him time to time. I was enlisting his service,

however, for the task at hand. Lucky for me, he was a receiving

worker, meaning he cleaned the bullpens that niggas had to go

in while waiting to be transported to court. That green uniform

was his pass to move around the jail freely.

Naheem had no problem getting on my team because

Eisha and her man were double charging him for buks and 30s. I

made him my LT since he was the only nigga in the jail I trusted.

He proved he was down when he got me Eisha's schedule,

section, and all the niggas she was fucking. To be honest, Eisha

was a hoe. I don't know how, but this plan was going have to

work without me fucking her; I might get something from her

slut ass. She was what me, Moshi, and our older brother Purnell call a termite. Purnell was Eboni's older brother that sold weed upstate, but he came down so fucking much that nigga got an apartment over in Dutch Village. Anyway, when I entered BCDC on a Sunday, I had my plan in place and ready to get this shit over with. I was about to take down one of the biggest smuggling rings in Maryland with a two-man team and good dick.

# Good Girlz With Hood Habits

Eboni

I woke up to the smell of chocolate chip pancakes, turkey sausages, fresh strawberries, and Trevor's head in between my legs. It was Sunday, and my man was home.

"Oh, shit Snoo, yesssssssss don't stop, eat this box, oh my goddddddd."

I was screaming so loud I knew I woke everybody in the house up, but I wasn't going to stop him from having Eboni a'la mode. Trevor's dick was to me what a pacifier was to a newborn. I went to bed with his dick in my mouth, and it was my alarm clock in the morning. Craved his dick was an understatement; I lived for that man.

"Ride my face, Eboni."

When Snoo laid down, instead of getting on his face, I jumped on his big black dick.

"Eboniiiiiiii," he stuttered.

"I know, Snoo, but I missed daddy dick so much, you want me to stop?" I asked while clenching and unclenching my pussy muscles around his dick.

# Good Girlz With Hood Habits

"Mmmmmm, no baby, don't stop, go ahead and get your dick." Snoo's eyes rolled into the back of his head as he palmed my ass like a basketball; he hated for me to go too fast or too slow. He wanted to enjoy the feeling of my warm wet box that was designed just for him. Five minutes into our sex session, I turned around on his dick and rode him cowgirl style. I was fucking my man into a frenzy... Knock, knock, knock.... "Mrs. Ballard, breakfast is ready..."

I was awaken by Maria, the morning maid at the Knights house. A fucking wet dream!

# Good Girlz With Hood Habits

Trevor

*Three months later......*

To infuriate an organized organization takes time, skill, patients and has many levels of difficulty. Not this one though; the shit was easy as fuck! First, Eisha was over charging niggas and under paying her soldiers. What women don't realize is pussy can only keep a man for so long, you need something else besides pussy to keep a man, and to my advantage, that was the only thing Eisha had to give these niggas. So, I used her one asset against her. I got Naheem to put word out that Eisha was a hoe and had fucked a few niggas on Nic section. Oh yeah, I knew about her nigga Nic, and I knew for a fact that he didn't realize Eisha was fucking his daughters God Father Terry, that information I was keeping to myself for the right moment. Don't get me wrong; Nic was cool just right now he was the competition, so that friendly shit went out the door. It was straight survival of the fittest right now. I had three more months in this shit, and I was done with this jail shit.

# Good Girlz With Hood Habits

"Yo, Naheem, you handled that for me?"

"Yeah, my nig Nic not fucking with her like that no more. He's questioning her loyalty, but yo did you know Nic and Redz knew each other?"

"Nah, Nic thinks Eisha is running shit with him as her muscle."

"Listen, my nigga, Nic fucking Syed down on J-section. My lil bro Trey sleep down there; he heard Nic and Syed talking the other day. First off, Nic don't really fuck with ya people's like that. He knows she's a smut; second, we need to hit that last cell because that's the real trap house. Nic and Red Nose not only know each other, but they are working together to get all they can out of Eisha then kill her freak ass."

"Damn yo where you get all that shit from? This shit bigger than I thought, this some real-life soap opera shit."

"But yo, you ain't hear that shit from me. I'm out son."

"Good looking my nigga, call Leah she got something for you. I'm out." This jail shit is getting out of fucking hand.

# Good Girlz With Hood Habits

Eboni was about five months now with our twins. We found out it was a girl and boy combo, so we picked Brooklyn - Ski, and Harlem- Knight for their names. This pregnancy was a high-risk one because the doctors said Eboni's body had been through a lot at just 26 years old. The wild and crazy sex we did and all those pregnancies she's been through was tearing my poor baby's body down.

# Good Girlz With Hood Habits

Eboni

***Visiting Day......***

"Ballard!" screamed a CO.

Every Saturday, like clockwork, I sat across a table sitting in a hard-blue plastic chair for 60 minutes with my husband.

"Gm Mrs. Ballard," he said, walking over to the table with his white t-shirt, blue Levi's, and white air forces. Snoo looked like a nigga straight from the BX. We hugged and kissed for as long as we could before the CO said something. This visit was different though, today Moshi, and Mr. Knight were there.

"Man stop all that mushy bull shit," said Moshi.

"Man go to hell," joked Trevor. "Hey, pops," he greeted Mr. Knight with a hug.

"Hey Stink, can you go get me some snacks from the vending machine?"

"Sure, Snoo, you guys need anything?"

"No, we're good sis, just be careful." I walked away to give the

guys space and time to talk without me because when I came

back, I wanted my man to myself.

# Good Girlz With Hood Habits

## Trevor

When Eboni left, I got straight to business.

"What's so important that you had to come up here, Pops?"

"T, you know I love you like my very own son, so know what I'm about to ask you isn't something I wouldn't ask Moshi."

"I know, pops, what's up?"

"I need you to end Nic's lease."

"Wait a minute, pops, you are talking about murking a nigga? I'm in here for DUI, not murder; that's not my bag. Fuck no! Y'all got the jail back and making money again what the fuck you mean dead that nigga?"

"Chill T, take some of that base out your fucking chest. Some personal shit happened, Nic put a hit out on Pop's brother, you remember Uncle Bobbie, right? Well, he is dead now, found in the parking lot of that McDonalds on White Ave," Moshi said with tears in his eyes.

"Damn Moshi, Bobbie was an uncle to me too, but yo, I'm no killer. Fuck I look like killing a nigga in jail. Yo, I get caught; I'm never coming home. Fuck this petty ass six months bullshit. I'm going to be sitting for life. What about my kid's nigga? What about my wife?"

"Nigga don't you think we've thought of all that shit. Pops didn't say you had to be the one that does it, just make sure the shit gets done."

"Pops, are y'all for real?"

"Son, I know it's a lot, but you're the only one right now that can get close to him; he's not coming home, so I can't get to him on the streets. I'm asking a lot, I know, but I'll triple what I already placed in your account."

"This some crazy-ass wild ass Wild Wild West shit you read in books, man look I need to think about this shit. This shit is going above the call of brotherhood. I'm putting my family and freedom on the line. This shit a little too deep for me."

"Trevor, I understand your resistance with what I need you to do, but you see my dilemma, right? He's locked up and will be for the next 10-15 years living, getting rich while my niece had to bury her father, my damn brother! You're my only chance at vengeance."

# Good Girlz With Hood Habits

"But pops, what about my freedom, kids, wife. What am I supposed to tell Eboni if something goes wrong?"

"Nothing will go wrong. You're smart and have learned the jail in your short time of being there, use your resources."

"One million."

"What?"

"Pops, you taught me better than anybody, and if I'm to put my life on the line, I need more than a couple hundred grand."

"The student has become the teacher, respect. I'll wire it into your account once the job is done."

"Nah, I want half now in cash the other half when the job is done all cash, though."

"No problem, Trevor, I understand a man in your position has the upper hand, family or not, you're about your business. I respect that."

"You taught me well, Pops."

"Moshi, take five out the safe and take it to the house while Eboni is not there."

Right on cue, Eboni walked back with an arm full of snacks.

Page 215

"Damn, sis, you hungry?"

"Oh, shut up, you try being pregnant with twins and see if you don't eat like a pig."

"Leave my baby alone nigga."

"Man shut up, with your box headed ass."

We joked and talked for the rest of the hour visit, then they left, and I walked to my cell, putting together a bulletproof plan. I couldn't believe I agreed to kill a nigga, but on the flip side, this was a big ass payout. I went back and forth in my head if I should tell Eboni what was about to go down, fuck no, she'll kill my ass for even thinking about it. I'm sure she's going to wonder why there was a shit load of cash in our damn house, though.

# Good Girlz With Hood Habits

## Eboni

Trevor didn't know I heard the whole conversation between him and the Knights men. I knew something was going on but didn't know it was this extreme. I was pissed that my husband was being pulled into this life. I tried hard to keep Snoo out of the streets. My family had ties in this street world no one knew about. Even Poppa Knight knew the meth of my family but never put two and two together. However, after hearing the bull shit Poppa Knight had my husband about to do, I knew I would have to dig back into my old life so my husband wouldn't have to get his hands dirty. Snoo didn't know all of my family history or the connections we had, so I had to move in silence.

First things first, I needed to get a message to Naheem. Naheem wasn't just my best friend's baby father; he was also my God Brother. Our God Mother was a badass bitch that taught us this street shit at a young age. No one knew we were family, and that's how our God Mother wanted it to be. So, whenever the other was in trouble or needed work done, no one would put the two of us together. I hooked him up with

# Good Girlz With Hood Habits

Leah so he could have a reason to be around, getting her pregnant was the icing on the cake, now I'm forever surrounded by a true hitter.

Getting to Naheem wasn't going to be easy without raising an eye or two. I had to get Purnell involved, but he was so loyal to Trevor that he might say something to his ass; there was only one other way, and I really didn't want to have to go through her because she was retired and off the grid, just calling her could be detrimental to her freedom. Still, my family needed it, plus I haven't seen her in forever! I was going to Florida to visit my G-mom.... Gisella Blanca.

I walked out of the jail in heavy thoughts. I didn't know much about "jail shit," and I didn't know Eisha freak ass was a boss. I thought she just fucked for money. All I know is that shit sounded like none of our damn business. I was sitting on the Knights porch when we got back from the visit at first, but the longer I sat, the angrier I got, so I got in my car and just drove. I ended up at Mr. Knight's nightclub back in the city on Pulaski Hwy; I knew some of the bartenders and bouncers from the

# Good Girlz With Hood Habits

little company get together that Mr. Knight always invited us to.

By the time I was ready to put my lips on my second glass of

wine, Mr. Knight came snatching it out of my hand.

"Eboni, what are you doing? Do Trevor know where you are?"

"How the fuck he's going to know when his ass is locked up

plotting murder for your ass?"

"Eboni, you're drunk and pregnant, I'm taking you home."

"You're the one that got him out here being James Bond with

your damn 007 missions; you don't care about my family; all you

care about is your damn drug empire!"

With that, I threw my glasses across the bar. I was done

with everyone. I didn't care that I was making a complete fool of

myself; I was fucking hurt man.

"Eboni, go to my office!"

"No, but I'll take another drink, please."

Papa Knight picked me up and carried me to his back office all

the while I was kicking and cursing his ass out.

"Now you listen hear little girl, what you're doing is stupid,

you're five months pregnant with twins and in a bar, drinking acting like street trash, is this how you want your daughters to see you?"

I smacked him, "No, now you listen, I've been nothing but a good woman, wife, and mother. I smile and barely say two words against you, my husband, or your son, but this has gone too far! You're putting my husband's life on the line for what? I'm sorry about Uncle Bobbie, I really am. But my husband will not be the next picture on a R.I.P shirt. So, send Moshi to come get that damn money out my house and leave my family alone!"

With that, I walked out of his office and the club. I didn't want to go home, so I drove to my big brother's house that he had here in Baltimore. He wasn't in town, so I knew the place would be empty for me to be alone. I texted my aunt to let her know where I was. I stayed there until the following Friday; I didn't talk to Trevor, Mr. Knight, Moshi, or Mrs. Knight. I ignored everyone. I felt betrayed, and I know I could have taken it overboard, but I didn't care. I felt like a damn fool.

Ring, ring, ring

# Good Girlz With Hood Habits

I looked at the caller ID; it was Eisha. I didn't feel like talking to her, so I sent her to voicemail. That's strange Eisha never leaves voicemails.

"Man, fuck Eboni cry baby ass, I don't know what Trevor sees in her ass. She needs to hit that gym and stop having all them fucking babies. I swear next time I see that fine as man of hers, I'm straight fucking him. I'm tired of just sucking his dick. That shit big too, girl."

"Girl, you crazy, ain't that your cousin."

"So, fuck her, that high yella bitch never had to work a day in her spoiled ass life."

Eisha and her homegirls talked about me like I was a dog for three minutes before the voicemail caught her off. Damn, that's how bitches really feel? I wasn't even mad about the dick sucking; after everything I heard, I knew Trevor was using her to get to Nic. I'm just glad he didn't fuck her freak ass. However, it was time I let the Brooklyn, NYC, be shown to these dumb ass Baltimore bitches.

"Hello, Mr. Knight, can you meet me at my brother's house this evening? I need to talk to you about something."

"Eboni, honey, is everything okay? Why aren't you taking Trevor's calls?"

"Mr. Knight, I just need you to come to see me, and please don't tell Trevor."

"Okay, Lady E, I'll be there around four."

"Thank you, pops."

That gave me just enough time to wipe my damn tears and put a plan in action.

Knock, knock, knock

"What's wrong, Lady E? Are you okay? Do you need anything."

"I'm fine, pops, I called you over here cause if my husband is going to do this, it's going be on my terms. First, I'm going to apologize for putting my hands on you, but I won't apologize for what I said. You put my husband in a fucked-up situation because of his loyalty to you."

"I can respect that, Eboni, and of course, Trevor doesn't have to do this, there will be no love lost."

"No, you've been good to our family, and we love you like our own father, Trevor's loyalty is one of the reasons I love him, so here's the deal. Once this deal is over, I need Trevor to be free. I know you have the powers, moves, and connections to make that happen. I don't care how you do it; I don't care if he only has two weeks left, as soon as this deal is over, I want my man out! And I need $100,000.00, all cash."

"Eboni, you do know Trevor is being well compensated for his services, right?"

"Yes, pops, I am aware of what you paid and will pay my husband, but a wise woman once told me your husband belongs to you. These streets are only renting him, so make sure they pay one hell of a leasing fee."

He chuckled, "I see you've been talking to my wife. You kind of remind me of her, Clarren was always two steps ahead of me."

"So, you can see why this meeting doesn't need to be discussed with my husband, correct?"

"Yes, boss," we both laughed.

"Eboni, you're an amazing woman, and Trevor is blessed to have you. Moshi will bring you the money tonight, and I'll talk to Ms. Lopez to see if we can get this ruling overturned."

"Thank you, Papa." I hugged him and walked him to the door.

When Papa Knight left, I called my best friend Leah and talked to her for a while. I didn't tell her much about what was going on, but I did tell her that I needed her and our other friend Krystal to fuck Eisha freak ass up. I would have done it myself, but clearly, I couldn't in the condition I was in being pregnant and all. After talking to Leah, Moshi finally came to the house around 8 pm.

"Hey, big bro."

"What's up, lil sis, pops told me to give you this bag. What's really going on, sis? Why you run away like that, you got my brother sick for real. You not answering his calls, the kids asking bout you, what the fuck is wrong with you?"

"Well, damn, I thought my daddy died years ago, and you and your brother both know why the fuck I flipped out. Don't play stupid, Darrell; it doesn't look good on you."

# Good Girlz With Hood Habits

"Oh, now I know you are bugging when the fuck we start going

by government names, Eboni Demetria Stanley-Ballard."

"Fuck you, Moshi," we both laughed. "Lil, big head half African

ass! Give me my damn bag." I snatched the bag out his hand.

"Sis, let me hit Krystal phat ass, you know I want her."

"Oh, hell, no, you not fucking up my friendship, you man whore,

plus you know she fuck with Roc short ass anyway."

"Man fuck that nigga. I'm going to get her red ass. Anyway, I'm

out. One!"

"Bye, Moshi."

"You have a collect call from Trevor Ballard at the Baltimore City

Detention Center, to accept this call dial 0." I pressed zero and

went in on Snoo.

"Have you lost your fucking mind? I don't care if the president

of the United fucking States asked you to do what Poppa asked

you, you better Obama fuck no."

"Stink, what are you talking about?"

"Snoo, don't play with me like I'm fucking dumb. I heard the

whole conversation at the visit."

Page 225

# Good Girlz With Hood Habits

"But stink."

"But stink my ass, now I know you're the man of this house, and as your wife, I will stand by your side with any decision you make for this family but Trevor, this shit is not us. I'm not married to John Gotti and Tony Mon fucking Tana. No, hell, no! I'm telling you this shit now; you try and do some stupid shit like that, and you won't have to worry about that little piece of change taking care of your family cuz your stupid ass won't have one."

"Eboni, listen, damn! And stop fucking cussing at me. I can't say much on this bluebird, but I'm straight, my hands won't get dirty."

"You sound so fucking stupid, if Papa Knight and Moshi so big and fucking bad tell them to get locked up and they take their monkey asses in that jail to do that shit. I can't believe you; you wait till now to want to start being a Billy fucking badass. Whatever Snoo just don't call me when your stupid ass serving life in a federal institution."

# Good Girlz With Hood Habits

I hung up. Oh, you thought I wasn't going to give him a piece of my mind. I love Snoo, no doubt, and I was ready to ride, but the shit he agreed to was stupid and reckless. Now the myth about my Godmother is she was killed back in 2012. Only Naheem, I, and her children knew she was still alive. Even our parents thought she was dead. Before I went to Florida, I needed to head back home to the BX. Stepping into my old apartment felt like home. I never got rid of my first apartment when I moved to Baltimore, my stepsister; Whitney subleased it from me during her last two years at NYC. Now my oldest niece Kaya lived in it.

"Hey, auntie, what are you doing here?"

"This is still my place; what are you doing here in the middle of the day? Why aren't you in class, and who's car is parked in my spot?"

"Ummmm, auntie, you gotta promise not to tell my daddy."

"Kaya, don't tell me you're fucking already damn! Who is he, tell him to come out here?"

"Well, auntie, he's umm a...."

# Good Girlz With Hood Habits

Before she could finish her sentence, Moshi's older brother came walking out the room with house slippers and a robe on like he lived in this bitch.

"Oh, hell no, Tash, your old ass fucking my niece. Nigga you like 40 or something."

"Real funny E, you know I'm only 28. Kaya is 19; it's not that big of a difference."

"Yeah, whatever nigga, all I know is Kaya if you fucking with a Knight, your ass shouldn't still be living in no damn one-bedroom apartment, it ain't cute walking around with a wet ass and empty pocketbook. Be smart, baby girl. I'm out. I'm staying at the W if you need me. And Tash buy my niece a damn car, or I'm telling.......Today!"

As I walked out, I heard him say, "Get dressed, we going to the dealer."

I met with my uncle Eddie. He was a cop at New York University and had connections with every damn body.

"Hey, Uncle Eddie."

"Hey Eboni, how's my favorite niece doing?"

# Good Girlz With Hood Habits

"I'm good unc just big, that's all; anyway, I came up here cause I need you to get all the info you can on the people on this list. I'm going back home Sunday, so it's a rush order."

"Eboni, it's six people on this list, including your cousin. That's a lot to do in 24 hours."

I poked my lip out and crossed my arms like the spoiled baby that I'm.

"Okay, Eboni, I'll see what I can do. On one condition."

"What's that, unc?"

"See you in church tomorrow."

He got up and walked away. Since I was in my hometown, I went to my old hairdresser to get my dobbie done. The Dominicans in Baltimore was cool, but I loved the way Susie made my hair look and feel.

"Hola señoritaaaaaaaaa," I screamed, walking into the shop.

"Oh, my goodness is that my mama seta."

"Yep, the one and only."

"On no, no honey who's been playing in my hair, come sit in my chair este pelo es un desastre, que diablos?"

# Good Girlz With Hood Habits

We laughed and talked for hours. We talked about her kids and we exchanged pictures of our families and when the shop closed, we went to Justin's for Cheesecake.

"Girl, I heard Trevor was locked up. What the fuck is that about?"

"He got a DUI and has to do six months."

"Girl, you know your cousin is supposed to be a part of like one of the biggest drug empires in the jail."

"Yeah, I heard that bitch supposed to be a boss, but girl, how you know all that?"

"You know my youngest son's father in Rikers, word travel fast in jail. But listen, the nigga she working with is suspect, think his name Redz or something, but he supposed to be an informant for the state, so tell Trevor to stand clear of his rat ass."

"Girl, you know my square ass man don't be in no shit, he just doing this lil weekend shit, then that's it."

"I hear you, baby girl, and we both know that's not true; tell him to be careful just in case."

# Good Girlz With Hood Habits

We finished eating; then I went back to my hotel. My oldest brother Purnell was knee-deep in the drug game and had connections in a lot of places. I sat with him the rest of the night, strategizing a plan to get Nic, my cousin, and that nigga Redz hit without our names coming up. I left New York with a whole new attitude, my family was at risk, and I had to get us out of this shit.

# Good Girlz With Hood Habits

Trevor

I was sick, no real talk, I couldn't eat, I couldn't sleep, I was throwing up. I missed my fucking woman; she was gone a whole week and wouldn't answer my calls. I had Moshi, Papa Knight, and Purnell texting, dm, inbox messaging everything and she never replied. I didn't want to even try to murk Nic bitch ass; my head wasn't right. I mostly stayed sleep all day and night. I talked to Naheem for a minute, but that was it. I was about to break out of this damn jail until Poppa Knight told me he had spoken to her. I was relieved and able to focus back on the task at hand.

Eisha came and got me from the gym around 3:30 in the morning. Since I have been here, I let her suck my dick, but I never fucked her for two reasons, Eboni would kill me, and I didn't have any rubbers. I didn't trust that hoe as far as I could throw her. When Eisha came to get me, her face was fucked up.

"Damn, Eisha, what happened to your face?"

"One of these clown ass niggas told Nic I was fucking around, and he beat me up."

# Good Girlz With Hood Habits

I know I was cruddy for thinking this, but in the back of my head, I was dying laughing, that's what that hoe gets.

"Are you serious that nigga put his hands on you? That's some fluke shit." I really didn't give a damn; Nic's days were numbered. "Yo Eisha I know it's none of my business, but you need to let that nigga go, fuck type of man is that to put his hands on a female."

"I know T; I'm done with his ass after that. I'm not a fucking punching bag. I'm getting one of these niggas to murk his ass, I swear."

"Eisha, I got you, I never liked his ass anyway."

"Nah T, you not bout that life, I'm good, I wouldn't want you to get caught up in my drama and get jammed then my cousin would never forgive me."

"Man, fuck what you are saying, you on my team too. I got it, just let me put some shit together, and he'll be gone before you know it."

"You sure!"

"Girl, stop that shit, come on I got you, now come suck on daddy dick so I can go to sleep."

"T, when you going let me ride that big motherfucker? I mean, you get a nut every day, but what about me? Don't you want to feel this wet shit? I know I can do better tricks than my boring ass cousin."

"First of all, Eisha, watch your fucking mouth, what we do is between you and me. Matter fact, you can't even suck my shit tonight. Dismissed."


*Visit Day.......*

"Bae, where you been. I'm sorry, stink, I won't do this shit if it's going have you disappearing and shit."

"Snoo shut up; you're going to do it anyway; shit has changed, though."

Astonishment wasn't even close to the feeling I was having listening to my wife describe this malicious criminal over the top-secret agent mission she was trying to send me on.

# Good Girlz With Hood Habits

"Eboni, are you serious? You really are agreeing to me doing this and adding onto the body count."

"Yes, I am. Now Eisha, you don't really have to worry about, I'll handle her myself. Snoo, I know you're using her to infuriate her organization. I don't care to know what exactly you and she are doing. Just know I know. She's fucking with another guy in the North building. Over the phone, she refers to him as Polo, I don't know his real name yet, but I can tell based on the calls, he has some green pass or something like that, it allows him access to the whole jail. Eisha wants her business back and will use him to get to you and your squad. Whoever kills the other first, she's going to turn the other one over to the authorities."

"Stink, how do you know all this shit?"

"It's a lot about my family, you don't know Snoo, and I'm not sure if you're ready to know, it's rather complicated."

"We'll uncomplicate it, Eboni, I'm your husband now, so what else do I need to know?"

"For starters, my family has tides to both the Mexican and Black Cartel. My dad wasn't in the government's Army but more like a general in Gisela Blanca's drug cartel. She's actually my

godmother, and when I turn 30, I'll inherit a rather large part of

her empire."

"Eboni, get the fuck out of here, you joking, right? Here we are

struggling day to day, but you want me to believe you're the

princess of one of the largest drug empires in the late 70s. Let

me find out your dad was Daddy Pope or some shit. Is he the

leader of B13?"

"My dad's security clearance is classified, and you don't have to

believe who my family is just know I know my shit. And you got

two weeks to carry this mission; these will be the last two

weeks you spend as a resident of BCDC, so you better get ready

to carry out this damn mission. *Welcome to the T.E.A.M* Snoo, I

hope you're ready." And with that, she left me sitting in the

visitor's room.

I hope you guys enjoyed meeting each character. Their stories are far from over. Be on the lookout for;

*Welcome to the T.E.A.M*

*Kei's to da Bankz*

*Something About Them "Green" girls.*

*Coming Soon*

CPSIA information can be obtained
at www.ICGtesting.com
Printed in the USA
LVHW031646110121
676219LV00004B/679

9 780578 780054